SysML in Action with Cameo Systems Modeler

Implementation of Model Based System Engineering Set

coordinated by
Pascal Roques

SysML in Action with Cameo Systems Modeler

Olivier Casse

ELSEVIER

First published 2017 in Great Britain and the United States by ISTE Press Ltd and Elsevier Ltd

ISTE Press Ltd
27-37 St George's Road
London SW19 4EU
UK

www.iste.co.uk

Elsevier Ltd
The Boulevard, Langford Lane
Kidlington, Oxford, OX5 1GB
UK

www.elsevier.com

Notices

Knowledge and best practice in this field are constantly changing. As new research and experience broaden our understanding, changes in research methods, professional practices, or medical treatment may become necessary.

Practitioners and researchers must always rely on their own experience and knowledge in evaluating and using any information, methods, compounds, or experiments described herein. In using such information or methods they should be mindful of their own safety and the safety of others, including parties for whom they have a professional responsibility.

To the fullest extent of the law, neither the Publisher nor the authors, contributors, or editors, assume any liability for any injury and/or damage to persons or property as a matter of products liability, negligence or otherwise, or from any use or operation of any methods, products, instructions, or ideas contained in the material herein.

MATLAB$^{®}$ is a trademark of The MathWorks, Inc. and is used with permission. The MathWorks does not warrant the accuracy of the text or exercises in this book. This book's use or discussion of MATLAB$^{®}$ software or related products does not constitute endorsement or sponsorship by The MathWorks of a particular pedagogical approach or particular use of the MATLAB$^{®}$ software.

For information on all our publications visit our website at http://store.elsevier.com/

British Library Cataloguing-in-Publication Data
A CIP record for this book is available from the British Library
Library of Congress Cataloging in Publication Data
A catalog record for this book is available from the Library of Congress
ISBN 978-1-78548-171-0

Printed and bound in the UK and US

Contents

Foreword

When Olivier Casse first approached me to write a foreword for his much-anticipated new book *SysML in Action With Cameo Systems Modeler*, I was both delighted to hear from him and honored that such an experienced practitioner had written a complete and thorough text about one of the "core" No Magic solutions. The new book clearly and succinctly explains how to use Cameo Systems Modeler to support model-based systems engineering (MBSE) with SysML. Olivier's book is not a tutorial, but rather a generic methodology and process book. What is also worth noting is our long-standing relationship with Olivier Casse, whom we have known for many years. His strong ties to the French technology community, and being based in France, gives him a unique European perspective, especially in light of the fact that his thirty-five years of experience ranges from engineering roles to sales and to enterprise consulting. Olivier, in every way, embodies the very best qualities of a systems modeling expert, and he brings this unique talent to his clear, concise writing style in this latest effort in the pages that follow. More and more, No Magic's European clients emphasize the growing importance MBSE is playing in a wide range of industries, and France is one of the leading countries in adopting MBSE. We know Olivier acknowledges this importance, so apparent from the rapid European adoption of MBSE in the automotive, transportation, aerospace, defense, and manufacturing sectors.

As President and CEO of No Magic and an Engineering alumni of Purdue University, I was recently elected to serve for a fifth term on the Board of Directors of Object Management Group (OMG). For almost a decade I have established close ties to this important software standards organization. In many ways this relationship with OMG has influenced No Magic and the solutions we offer, making us the most standards-compliant in the industry. Everyone at OMG has seen the sustained interest in SysML and recognizes the exponential growth of MBSE.

Perhaps it is a coincidence, or excellent timing, that the release of Olivier's new book comes on the 20th anniversary of the release of No Magic's award-winning software MagicDraw, our core modeling platform, which is the foundation on which Cameo Systems Modeler is developed. I found Olivier's appropriate section on the Key Elements of Modeling very timely, and a welcoming foundation for those who are newer to modeling and want to set the stage for what's to come in subsequent chapters.

I am delighted that *SysML in Action* draws the reader through an in-depth view and explanation of the role model execution plays in system simulation using Cameo Simulation Toolkit, (the only out-of-the-box co-simulation product in the market). In this section, Olivier emphasizes the real-world value of model-based system simulation, i.e. to gain system understanding without manipulating the real system, either because it is not yet defined or available, or because it cannot be executed directly due to cost, time, resources or risk constraints. From my personal experience, other MBSE books focus on model creation, yet Olivier goes beyond that in his book by demonstrating how the use of models brings value in typical engineering activities.

Having recently returned from an extended three-week trip to China and Japan, where I kicked off a series of No Magic in-depth MBSE days for the burgeoning Asian market, I was struck by the many ways the Japanese and Chinese are now firmly embracing MBSE. This market, like those in North America and Europe, sees the importance of MBSE and understands the benefits of employing this modeling discipline in their processes. After each session, I was surrounded by interested attendees wanting to learn more. My only regret is that we did not have Olivier's new book at the podium. We could envision giving a copy of *SysML in Action with Cameo Systems Modeler* to each and every one of the hundreds of attendees with whom we personally shared our MBSE story. Olivier's new book tells this story with the detail and clarity desired by this audience. This underscores once again why MBSE is important to professionals and to their enterprises, no matter where they are in the world.

No Magic acknowledges the importance of method by the recent introduction of MagicGrid, a No Magic MBSE methodology and framework which is well presented by Olivier in his text. Olivier explains that MagicGrid is important because there is a need for a method/framework to define the modeling process and ensure the systematic use of SysML. MagicGrid is important to this discussion because it allows an organization to take advantage of their current process and culture. With MagicGrid, adoption of MBSE is faster. Companies can begin with requirements or use cases or any of the SysML diagrams. Olivier's MagicGrid discussion underlines the need for this graphical notation and provides additional context for model integrity, reusability and interoperability, all integral to MBSE in real-world applications. After all, as I mentioned earlier, this is first and foremost a methodology and process book. It is different and unique when compared to other MBSE books we've encountered. Olivier has been generous with his use of clear models and an excellent, highly readable visual style throughout. The reader is in for a pleasant surprise, as this book is much visually richer than other books on the subject I have seen.

There is another facet of this story taking place in France that needs to be told as well. The Education Nationale for French Lycées made the decision to bring a nationwide model-based systems engineering approach to French high schools which focuses on engineering and natural sciences. The search was on for a software solution ideally suited to this younger audience as well. The schools based their choice of what solution to adopt based on several criteria, including ease of use and standards compliance to SysML. A nationwide evaluation took place, and the recommendation from the evaluation team was No Magic's MBSE solution, consisting of MagicDraw with the SysML plugin as the preferred choice. Today more than 500 lycées now use No Magic's MBSE software for their MBSE education. No Magic also receives frequent requests from colleges and universities in France seeking MagicDraw and Cameo Systems Modeler. This is simply the natural progression of students from the lycées graduating to the university level who are already familiar with MagicDraw models and Cameo Systems Modeler. We expect Olivier's new book in French to be a popular companion text among French engineering students and faculty and critical to MBSE adoption in France.

The groundwork for MBSE using No Magic has been taught early on and comes naturally I expect. While other books on the shelves focus on language or method, Olivier's book delivers more detail on using Cameo Systems Modeler. As a result, it excels in both its practicality as a teaching guide and its ease by which students can learn by example.

The story we tell over and over again, and the one that Olivier dramatically paints throughout his book, is that MBSE is smart engineering. Why? Because MBSE adds real engineering rigor to the Systems Engineering process. I look forward to the release of the English translation of this book this autumn. The English version will be a great addition and an ideal reference guide for workshops regardless of locale.

I can say with 100% assurance that now more than ever, MBSE is one of the most important topics of discussion in the modeling industry. With our highly connected world, MBSE works to simplify the complexity. I see this strong movement to MBSE in our customer engagements, customer questions and the number of MBSE training requests we receive each day. We also see the rapid growth of Model Based Systems Engineering at trade shows we sponsor and attend, within professional organizations, through our affiliation with INCOSE, the International Council on Systems Engineering, and at the four quarterly OMG technical meetings each year. INCOSE, the world's most significant association of engineers, presents MBSE as the future of System Engineering (SE), and looks forward to MBSE becoming a common practice synonymous with SE.

It is our hope that industry professionals will make available copies of "SysML in Action With Cameo Systems Modeler" for those new to modeling and simulation and to their project leads and others on their staff. Systems engineering thought leaders will find this book of great value as they look for ways to adopt and implement smart engineering to benefit their enterprise. These professionals, from those new to modeling to experienced engineers, will discover with great clarity in the pages of Olivier's book that the use of SysML and MBSE is mission-critical, providing better business outcomes. Olivier's book, while telling the MBSE story, does our modeling community the greatest good. *SysML in Action With Cameo Systems Modeler* gives readers a smart, robust and intuitive learning tool for all audiences. Today, it is more important than ever that we endeavor to define, track and visualize all aspects of systems in the most standards-compliant SysML models and diagrams.

Gary DUNCANSON
President and CEO
No Magic, Inc.
Object Management Group Board of Directors

Preface

Objectives of this book

During initial discussions in the creation of this series of books with Pascal Roques, where each book will detail the implementation of a particular tool, the following reflections quickly arose: we will write a new book on Systems Modeling Language (SysML), so what is missing from existing works?

What has not been written about SysML and its implementation? What innovative stance do we give to it?

This is how it began.

We will use quite a few definitions (or summaries of standards) in this book (except those of the SysML language itself), yet some are essential. However, we will begin by defining what a methodology is.

A methodology is a set of related processes, methods and tools used to support a specific discipline. SysML is primarily a toolbox which the system engineer will dip into in order to use the elements at his disposal best suited according to the project, the context and of course its use and its industry. We will return to this later when justifying the choice of a diagram over another in our model.

This toolkit, as anticipated by the OMG (Object Management Group), does not include a standard approach whereby this diagram should be used at this stage of the project, to describe this part, at such and such a stage or level. One of the contributors to the definition of SysML, INCOSE, have proposed a state of the art methodology in systems engineering and IEEE-15288, the pivotal standard in SE called OOSEM (Object-Oriented Systems Engineering Method).

Our approach, while being in line with that of INCOSE, is simplified and is based on the basic principles of MBSE (Model Based System Engineering) which governs the work within the OMG on the different methodologies used in the industry.

This book will use CSM (Cameo Systems Modeler) from No Magic to (1) illustrate the modeling of the application example used as a guideline to (2) describe a generic approach, as well as (3) recalling the key concepts of the SysML language.

It is the set of these three connected aims which will allow us to illustrate a scenario using an MBSE approach.

No Magic supports several methodologies, including Magic Grid, developed in-house. Its objective is to illustrate how to adapt a tool to a project-oriented approach, to its domain and to different stakeholder businesses whether based on a standard or entirely proprietary (which is rather rare).

With this approach, No Magic offers to manage the four pillars: Requirements, Behavior, Structure and Parametrics using three abstraction levels: problem in black box, in white box, and then a solution, resulting in eleven steps, as illustrated in Figure 1, MagicGrid Framework for MBSE.

To complete this set, where the SysML notation is already chosen, there is the method described later in this book and there is also the selection of the modeling tool (among other system engineering tools) which will become relevant.

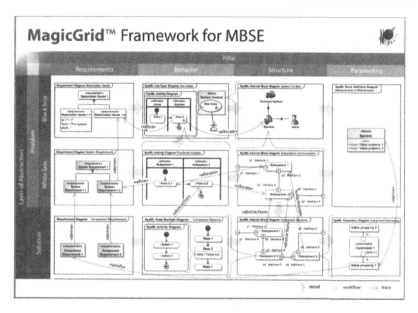

Figure 1. *MagicGrid approach by No Magic. For a color version of this figure, see www.iste.co.uk/casse/sysml.zip*

Some tool publishers propose (or recommend) a methodology deemed to be adapted to all projects, occupations and problems ... It is of course impossible that this methodology meets the requirements of all scenarios, and even if this were the case, the partners in a complex project cannot be given a different tool for each new project. It is therefore essential that the methodology is relatively independent of the tools, just as the tools must be able to support the chosen methodology.

We will discuss the MBSE approach, serving as a guide, a little later and, by using the models, we will see that a better formalization by the reduction of certain ambiguities inherent in the use of the natural language optimizes communication between the parties of a project. This approach aims to cover the different levels used in a System Engineering approach, from the requirements to validation, iteratively. The entire product lifecycle is not necessarily addressed by SysML modeling but the models largely cover these steps, especially the definition phases, where precision will reduce the risks and the costs, while improving the quality and brand image of the company leading the project.

We will not deal directly in this book with the ontology allowing us to share knowledge by structuring the concepts describing a domain, even if our application example comes from the automotive world, our objective being that reading this book is possible regardless of the professional domain of the reader.

Our methodology is simplified yet very representative of what an industrial project can require for its success based on the state of the art and the different standards in force.

NOTE.– This is not a tutorial; we will not focus too deeply on all the functionalities of the tool, only those that are considered significant, with particular emphasis on how CSM supports SysML modeling. We will comment on the model obtained in the following areas:

– context level summary (what we need to do there);

– an analysis of the procedure;

– screenshots;

– tips and tricks, other possible options.

It is not our intention to present all of the SysML modeling elements available in this toolkit (there are other reference works and the standard specification for this); we will instead focus on the key items from a practical perspective using both the case study and the modeling tool.

Structure of this book

The structure of this section will give you an idea of which chapter to consult according to your requirements, level of knowledge of the SysML language and your expertise in the CSM tool.

The main part of this book, which constitutes its original value compared to other books already available on SysML, includes a case study focused on the heart of a modeling tool, where we will comment on the model obtained by following our approach in Chapter 4 "Case Study".

However, if you are not very familiar with SysML or wish to refresh your knowledge, Chapter 1, "SysML: Object Management Group (OMG) Systems Modeling Language", will serve as a reference to SysML. A brief overview of the MBSE approach is also provided, which is key in the structuring of our project and necessary before we get to the heart of the matter!

Chapter 2, "About Cameo Systems Modeler", will provide you with practical information about Cameo Systems Modeler. Of course, some aspects are very specific, but often the operating procedures are relatively common to most modeling tools that can be used industrially.

Chapter 3, "Example", describes the topic of the example chosen, which is a centralized locking system for a motor vehicle.

Finally Chapter 5, "Beyond Modeling", will complete Chapter 3 on supplements to the modeling itself in order to derive all the benefits of the MBSE approach, for example V & V.

The index at the end includes many of the terms used, from the SysML keywords to system engineering terminology.

Acknowledgements

I would like to warmly thank:

− Eric Andrianarison (Business Consultant at Siemens PLM Software) who I initially met at Valeo, as a client.

− Stéphane Badreau (Consultant Manager at Compliance Consulting), with whom I regularly collaborate.

− Pascal Roques (Trainer/Senior Consultant at PRFC) who motivated me to write this book and whose courses I often take part in.

I also thank No Magic for providing the licenses for their Cameo tool and for their support. I made repeat requests to the support team, congratulations for their efficiency. I also had the opportunity to reuse a sharing forum open to clients as well as to curious individuals, discovered several years ago during my introduction to this tool, in which the community listened and shared its knowledge.

Creating a project based on SysML is a challenge and I wanted to highlight this having supported users of tools that rival No Magic for several decades... Thank you also to everyone else who enriched my experience. Finally, thanks to my wife Nadine for her support.

Olivier CASSE
September 2017

SysML: Object Management Group (OMG) Systems Modeling Language

1.1. Background

SysML is the result of a desire to establish a modeling language common to the stakeholders in a complex project of system engineering as of January 2001. Previous available approaches had great disparity, that is to the level of the languages and the tools, not promoting communication, maintenance etc.

Moreover, the Unified Modeling Language (UML) language, which had already been available at the time for over several years, was accessible on a large number of modeling tools. Some projects have tried to use UML as a means of system modeling. Unfortunately, its strong computing connotation and the lack of certain concepts (traceability of requirements for example) were a hindrance to the success of UML in Systems Engineering.

A consortium consisting of mainly American and European members has been created within the OMG with industrialists, mainly in the field of space and aeronautics, tool publishers, as well as academic organizations or groups of experts in the field, including the International Council on Systems Engineering (INCOSE), which we will discuss later.

Figure 1.1. *Official logo of OMG SysML. For a color version of this figure, see www.iste.co.uk/casse/sysml.zip*

1.2. What is SysML?

SysML is a modeling language consisting of a toolbox offering several ways to describe a complex system. SysML also proposes, in a Model-Based Systems Engineering (MBSE) framework, documenting a system from different points of view or perspectives, in order to make the description accessible to target readers.

SysML is not a method, no specific approach is proposed by the OMG for its implementation.

SysML reuses a subset of UML 2 and extends it to address the additional requirements of system engineering.

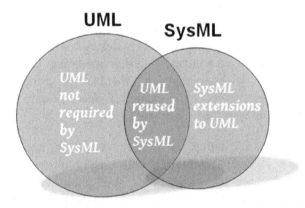

Figure 1.2. *SysML is both a subset and an extension of UML 2*

The part of UML reused for SysML is generally known as UML4SYSML.

We will see that many UML2 diagrams are repeated without any changes, or with few minor additions, which was one of the objectives of the OMG whereby tool publishers proposed a modeler that facilitated modifications; all SysML modeling tools are indeed based on a UML core, specialized for SysML through a dedicated profile.

The version of SysML described in this book is V1.5, which was the official version at the time of the publication of this book.

1.3. System Engineering in a nutshell

We will focus solely on aspects related to SysML, voluntarily omitting the other aspects (economic, commercial, regulatory, etc.), since they are beyond the context of this book.

System engineering is a multidisciplinary approach designed to enable the production of successful systems.

Figure 1.3. *Product Lifecycle*

This approach focuses on defining the customer needs and the functionalities necessary for the proper functioning of a system. These needs and expectations must be validated as early as possible in the development cycle, documenting the requirements and then carrying out the design and validation of the system, taking into account the whole topic to be covered: operational aspects, performance, testability, manufacturing constraints, costs and delays, training and support and ultimately disposal.

Several standards govern good Systems Engineering practices, in particular IEEE-15288, as well as EIA 632 and IEEE 1220. The main reference will be to IEEE-15288, for example highlighting these few key steps:

– specifications, interviews and customer requirements;

– defining the stakeholder need process;

– technical specifications;

– requirements analysis;

– definition of the preliminary system;

– design process.

1.4. Advantages of System Engineering

The following is a non-exhaustive list of the main benefits of using a system engineering approach. First, complying with the requirements given for a product ensures an increase in quality by implementing the verification and validation principle as early as possible. Then, mastering the complexity, through modeling and simulation, the decomposition of the system serving as a common basis for the development of the system (single and unified platform), exchanges and collaborative work.

Some advantages also derive from the objectives that will be set for modeling, in particular, an improvement in communication by speaking the same language, or more specifically an approved vocabulary and relevant semantics. For this, a common glossary will be of valued assistance, for natural language specifications or those documented by models. Good communication also means improved collaboration and interaction and a more flexible adaptation to change.

Finally, both an objective and an advantage, reusing existing artifacts (assets) will be possible.

Nevertheless, impact analysis, the reduction of development costs, reduction of time-to-market and an overall increase in quality are also worth mentioning.

1.5. The MBSE approach

The MBSE is based on a more comprehensive approach that relies on models specific to system engineering applications. This approach emphasizes the use of models during the life cycle of systems engineering activities such as the analysis and verification of requirements, analysis and functional allocations, performance analysis, compromise studies, system design specifications and not to mention the testing. This approach has become very popular with system engineers who advocate the use of SysML as a rigorous standard visual modeling language for system engineering applications, as opposed to other model-driven approaches, often focusing on software development. The complete paradigm combines good practices in systems engineering and even methodology, but we will see that OMG does not recommend this. However, INCOSE proposes one for themselves, and some academic and industrial stakeholders, tool editors and experts also propose them.

The challenges in terms of processes are:

– A central design: The MBSE approach must position a system design model as the first artifact obtained and used throughout the System Development Life Cycle (SDLC).

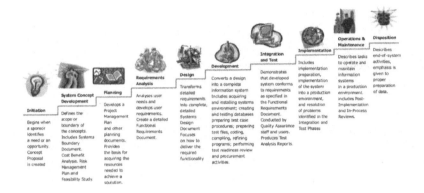

Figure 1.4. *System development life cycle phases*

The figure above provides a very comprehensive guide documented by the US Department of Justice:

– SDLC Compatibility: The MBSE process must support all SDLC phases: Requirements, Analysis, Design, Implementation, Integration and Test.

– Based on requirements with full V & V support: The MBSE process must fully support traceability of requirements including full verification and validation of all functional and non-functional requirements.

Moreover, it is desirable for the MBSE approach to have the following aims:

– Simplicity and rigor: The MBSE approach must be explained in a simple and rigorous way, so that system engineers can learn it and follow it easily.

– Support of free standards: The MBSE approach must support open standards for system design modeling and interoperability. These standards include, but are not limited to SysML, UML 2, XMI and AP233. These open standards should be used to specify the system design model and serve as a lingua franca, i.e. as a consensual notation, among system engineers and other stakeholders (software developers, electrical engineers, mechanics, not to mention customers, etc.).

NOTE.– Model-based specifications and simulation techniques have been associated with system engineering since its launch as an interdisciplinary engineering field, which can be traced back to work done by Bell Telephone Laboratories and the DoD (US Department of Defense) in the 1940s!

1.5.1. *V cycle and SE activities*

There is a large number of models that deal with methods linked to system engineering activities, such as: waterfall, V cycle and spiral models etc. The link between the chosen (and adapted) approach with System Engineering activities will only be illustrated through one of the most common cycles in the field of embedded systems: the V cycle, since this type of cycle (and its derivatives) is an excellent support to an MBSE approach.

Below is a figure illustrating how different SE activities are positioned using this cycle.

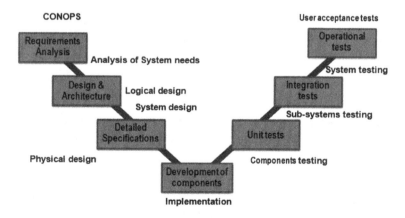

Figure 1.5. *Positioning of SE activities using the V cycle*

1.5.2. *Difference between a model and a drawing*

In other words, what are the significant advantages of using a model instead of an assembly of texts and images?

First, it is worth noting that a model can fulfil several objectives: for example, analysis, documentation, prototyping, verification and validation. We will discuss this on the following pages.

Several of these objectives will have, as a deliverable, a document or illustrations to complement a more general document, therefore we may think that the use of a tool such as CSM (Cameo Systems Modeler) or SysML will only be to produce documentation (from diagrams). This would mean forgetting the consistency that a model provides with existing links between all the elements constituting a model. See section 2.7.

A model in principle provides consistency, in particular by synchronizing the graphical symbols present in the diagrams with the elements of the repository – we will return to this later. Unfortunately, too often diagrams are copied/pasted from modelers to specification documents, without any validation or verification, restricting the use of these modeling tools to simple "super" drawing tools, even by trained personnel!

NOTE.– It is important to bear in mind that diagrams are only a representation of a point of view. A diagram usually contains only part of the elements constituting the model. In addition, the information present can be filtered on the display. For example, the compartments of a Block.

When modeling, we will only consciously manipulate the so-called concrete syntax, or immediate, roughly "draw boxes and arrows".

Beneath the concrete syntax, there is an equally important world!

The modeling tool, in line with the SysML standard, will use abstract syntax and the notation's semantics in order to fulfil the relations and other properties of the elements constituting the model.

Figure 1.6. *Abstract syntax and semantics*

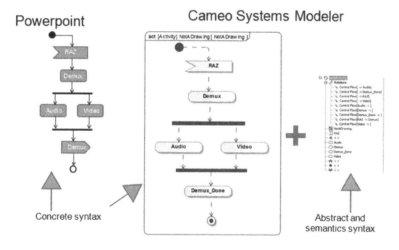

Figure 1.7. *Difference between a drawing and a model. For a color version of this figure, see www.iste.co.uk/casse/sysml.zip*

This abstract syntax and the associated semantics, even if not formally described by the OMG (for the action language, we will come back to this), is the key factor for computer calculations, simulation, traceability, etc. since publishers of modeling tools such as No Magic have completed SysML with variants of semantics based on the most common computer and business languages.

1.6. Scope and Objectives of the model

Following an MBSE approach by modeling a system must meet a need or more often a set of problems too complex to master by a verbal or documentary approach. It is out of the question to completely model a system in every detail. This project would be over (and would surely have been a failure) a long time ago. As modeling must be an improved communication vector, a powerful means of analysis, a better formalization of the system description, a mastery of system design and risks, it is therefore essential, even before the first mouse click, to define, in agreement with the other stakeholders, the intended objective of this modeling and hence the different groups of target readers. Indeed, the reading level will be in line with the level of expertise in the different business (financial, marketing, commercial, technical, analyst, architect, designer, tester, etc.).

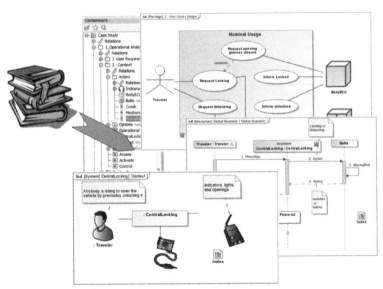

Figure 1.8. *Transition from a document based approach to modeling. For a color version of this figure, see www.iste.co.uk/casse/sysml.zip*

1.6.1. *Communication vector*

The advantage of sharing a model (even in paper form) no longer requires proof, in fact the propagation of the slightest modification in a model and in particular the guaranteed better consistency (compared to an image or text in a word processor) are all advantages in its favor.

1.6.2. *Powerful analysis*

Modeling tools have the ability to check the consistency of models for most functionalities, their completeness or even compliance with the standard used (such as SysML). The ability to evaluate any change gives you unparalleled flexibility, allowing you to consider any compromise, any request to change one of the constituents.

1.6.3. *Better formalization of the description of a system*

Even if SysML cannot be classed by traditionalists within the category of formal languages (only partially and rightly so), it remains true that this notation offers a certain rigor allowing a mutual understanding by the different partners in a project. This remains insufficient if an approach, a glossary and the verification rules are not put in place.

The main benefit of introducing an MBSE approach will be to propose a common multidisciplinary language. Of course each member of a project, according to his/her profession, uses vocabulary specific to his/her specialty, dedicated tools, adapted processes etc. SysML is not intended to replace these particularities, guaranteeing performance and efficiency, but to share an overall upstream level by minimizing the ambiguities inherent in the natural language during exchanges.

The figure below illustrates, according to the level of formalism, the ease of communication that is obtained:

1) mathematical expression, equations and requiring good expertise, (i.e. a known theorem);

2) graphical or algebraic representation, very precise, however its reading is not immediate, an interpretation of the same theorem …;

3) modeling with a state diagram: possibility of execution allowing validation/verification (we are close to the mathematical demonstration);

4) using the use case: this is more to do with structuring;

5) text description (extracted from the OMG SysML1.4 specifications).

NOTE.– 1 & 2 are coherent, 3, 4, 5 do not describe the theorem, they are simple examples.

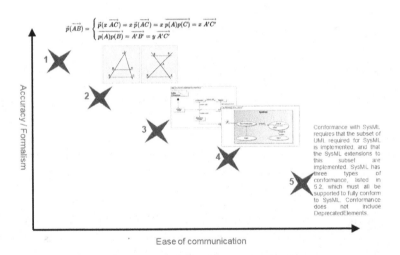

Figure 1.9. *Ease of communication according to the level of accuracy used. For a color version of this figure, see www.iste.co.uk/casse/sysml.zip*

1.6.4. *Mastering System Design*

The challenges of a complex project, often very long and costly, mean that controlling risks is crucial to its success, as is the sustainability of the companies realizing it. As SysML can be used in an MBSE approach, it is in a perfect position to improve its control, by bringing a certain rigor, the possibility of communicating in a less ambiguous way, to share, reuse and then document according to several points of view. Finally, the tools, and this is the case for CSM, offer simulation, analysis and prototyping opportunities allowing the greatest number of trades among the stakeholders to instrument the artifacts necessary for systems engineering.

1.6.5. *Other inputs*

Several successful projects have demonstrated a clear improvement in quality, better efficiency, knowledge capitalization and authentic reusability of project artifacts by means of a model-based approach.

Using a set of tools, key functionalities can be implemented, such as work sharing, user rights management, conflict prevention, up-to-date and accurate documentation.

There is also configuration management (versions, subdivisions etc.) in line with the tools generally used for development and manufacturing.

Finally, traceability, which is essential for current complex projects and can be easily equipped, simulation and animation capabilities, and virtual and/or rapid prototyping all contribute to the productivity and rigor of an effective MBSE approach.

1.7. Problem or solution?

In other words, which side of the "barrier" are you?

The limits of this barrier are extremely variable, as they depend on the field of application, the size of the project and the teams, expertise etc.

Are you on the side of the requiring entity, often referred to as the product manager, or the client i.e. the requestor? You define in principle the objective of the project, its timeframe, its budget, etc. The project manager is responsible for defining the product according to the perspectives of the customers and users, by expressing the need, following the realization and receipt of the product.

Or through a contract are you in charge of project management (prime contractor), so one of the suppliers? In this case it is your responsibility to ensure the smooth running of the project, its technical choices in order to achieve the objectives agreed with the requestors. The project manager is responsible for providing a solution, respecting the costs, the deadlines and the scope of the product, defining solutions, realizing it (producing or subcontracting) and ensuring the delivery, putting it into service and testing.

There will then be two facets, two categories of complementary requirements to be managed, depending on the level of responsibility and involvement during design or implementation of the system:

– user requirements, defined by stakeholders, to ensure that users' needs are taken into account. We refer to the PROBLEM;

– system requirements managed by analysts, architects, designers and testers, for whom the objective is that the product responds correctly to the needs expressed. We refer to the SOLUTION.

It should be noted that the boundary is never clear; the same entity may include several people performing roles in one category or in another.

In particular, there is almost never a completely new system, the project will probably inherit technological choices and constraints, part of the solution would be known.

The following table illustrates some differences between these two levels.

There are several transitions in the MBSE approach or more generally in the disciplines of system engineering. One of them lies in the transition from the domain of the problem to that of the solution. Indeed one of the upstream phases in engineering systems is engineering requirements. Many of these phases will be considered as transverse, the approach being generally iterative and, above all, numerous verifications and validations will be carried out, implying a strong and indispensable link to the requirements. These requirements, especially at the problem level, are expressed in text form. However, they can be supplemented by models, which of course we will address in this book.

Problem	Solution
User Requirements	System Requirements
Describing the problem and its context	Abstractly represent the solution
Describe the stakeholder expectations	Describe what the future system should do
Do not define the solution, but the context	Do not define design
Specify the quality of results	Specify quality of execution
Created by stakeholders	Created by system engineers

Table 1.1. *Differences between the problem and solution*

In summary, it is essential not to provide a model, but rather several sets of diagrams according to the categories of target readers, whether these are printed directly or integrated into a document, or that the models are used by the tools using simulation and animation capabilities as an interactive aid, or even generating an executable code in order to provide a prototype.

This prototype, for example associated with graphical tables, will allow the validation of system use scenarios, in line with the constraints (a category of requirements) or even to verify a healthy behavior.

1.8. SysML toolbox

SysML proposes nine diagrams for structuring the modeling. Some diagrams are taken from UML 2, four of which are taken as is, two are new, and the other three modified specifically to support systems engineering. The chart of requirements, the major contribution, falls between the two main categories grouping, on the one hand, the structural aspects and on the other hand, the behavioral aspects.

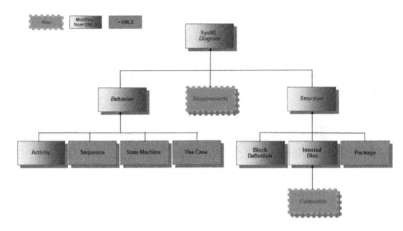

Figure 1.10. *The nine SysML diagrams. For a color version of this figure, see www.iste.co.uk/casse/sysml.zip*

The parametric diagram, which for a long time has been underutilized by the tools, helps specify constraints; these constraints can be exploited during a simulation (either by the integrated Cameo simulator which has its own solver, or by co-simulation with a dedicated tool), which reinforces its value during the verification and validation stages, or even in a trade-off study.

We will see that some diagrams can in fact be optional; the elements that make them up are sufficiently noteworthy to justify their use (and thus their definition) in the repository, without necessarily having to represent these elements in a diagram, for example the package diagram, or even that of the requirements.

NOTE.– It is important to consider these nine diagrams as carriers of the definition of elements of the SysML language, grouping together connected concepts, which make it possible to define elements; however, in the end a diagram will represent only a point of view, a particular perspective of the model. In other words, fulfilling the repository should not only be considered by diagrams; their creation independent of a diagram is highly recommended!

Finally we often talk about diagrams thinking about a schematic representation, and we will see that SysML provides a tabular representation, often much more efficient, especially for the readability of relations between elements.

NOTE.– The tabular representation serves as both a means of visualization and also as a means of creation, in particular, replacing the lines and arrows used in diagrams in order to establish these links graphically.

1.9. The SysML frame

This is a specificity with respect to UML since each SysML diagram must necessarily include a frame or box, delimiting the outline of the diagram. It consists of a header, indicating the type of diagram, the modeling element which is the default namespace, the qualified name, corresponding to the full path, with the diagram name.

For each diagram here are the possible namespaces:

- – act: activity
- – bdd: block, package or constraint
- – ibd: block or constraint
- – pkg: package or template
- – par: block or constraint
- – req: package or requirement
- – seq: interaction
- – stm: state machine
- – uc: package

uc [Package] Book[Missions]

Figure 1.11. *Example of a SysML reference box in Cameo*

Finally, the frame itself can be used to support certain elements, in particular the ports in an ibd, or even the parameter nodes in an activity diagram.

1.10. Stereotypes

The SysML profile, specializing UML in System Engineering modeling language, is itself a set of stereotypes. The idea of applying a stereotype to an element is to change its semantics, to specialize it by adding properties.

In CSM, a specific diagram has been provided for this purpose: the Profile Diagram. However, it is possible to create stereotypes outside this diagram, to save them in a specific package, thus enabling the customizations to be capitalized. The properties of a stereotype are called tags or labels.

1.10.1. *Labels (Tags)*

These labels or tags represent the properties of stereotypes, with two characteristics:

– tag Definition for their creation;

– tag Value for their use, instantiation.

Like any property, the Values are typed. Refer to section 1.15.3, which provides an example for more information.

In our model, several labels on the requirements are used to reflect the attributes of our repository and thus to be consistent on the one hand, and to inform certain values in the model, for example comments, on the other hand.

1.11. The requirements diagram (req)

This diagram makes it possible to take into account the requirements and especially their links with SysML modeling elements. Only two characteristics are specified: an identifier and a descriptive text (in addition to the name, common to any element of a SysML model). However, additional properties may need to be added so that the requirements imported in the SysML model match the requirements stored in an (external) requirement management tool.

1.11.1. Requirement

A requirement is a capacity or condition to be met by a system. The requirements are used to establish a contract between the client (or other stakeholders) and the stakeholder(s) in charge of the development and implementation of the system. A requirement may also appear on other diagrams to illustrate its relationships with other modeling elements.

When a requirement imbricates other requirements, all nested requirements are parts (see parts for a block) of the requirement that contains them. Destroying this induces the destruction of all contained requirements.

There are also several categories of requirements: functional, interfaces, performance, physical, business, company-related etc. which are clearly defined by the overall requirements, preferably before approaching the modeling.

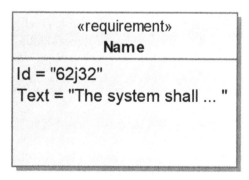

Figure 1.12. *SysML Requirement*

1.11.2. *Identifier*

This identifier will be unique and ideally retrieved from an external requirement management tool interfaced with CSM as it will serve to synchronize the properties of the requirements and their traceability links. Precise naming rules will be implemented to identify the level, such as type.

1.11.3. *Descriptive text*

This text is the essence of the requirement and its formulation, which will not be imparted in this book. However, the formulations related to the description of the problem will be considered "The user must be able to ...." and the solution "The system shall ..." as a template for the (good) drafting.

The text can be in raw format or in HTML, allowing better navigation and format.

1.11.4. *Extensions*

Many extensions are possible and desirable, in order to take the essence of an engineering requirements approach. In particular, the source, the development, the verification means, etc.

Compliance with the repositories in which these requirements are stored is essential, but it is not always desirable (including by another stakeholder) to access all attributes (confidential aspects, e.g. financial).

Refer to section 2.8, which provides an example for more information.

This example is based on the use of a stereotype and associated labels; this extension mechanism is applicable to other categories of SysML elements, such as Blocks, ports, activities etc.

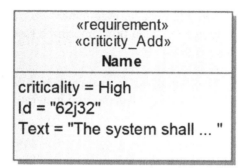

Figure 1.13. *An extended requirement with the attribute "criticality"*

1.11.5. *Links*

We will soon have an opportunity to study in detail the main links, particularly <<satisfy>> <<deriveReqt>> <<refine>> and <<verify>>.

<<deriveReqt>> is a dependency between two requirements, where the derived requirement is generated or inferred from the source requirement.

<<verify>> is a relation to a test case, described either by activity, state machine, or a sequence, a procedure used to verify a requirement.

<<satisfy>> is a link to connect an element of the model to a requirement, this link being a dependency, making it possible to satisfy this requirement. As with any other dependency, the direction of the arrow points from the element (the client) to the requirement (the provider).

<<refine>> is often used with other modeling elements, different from a requirement, to describe a textual requirement in more detail. For example, a Use Case may refine a requirement.

There are other links: <<copy>>, <<trace>> that can be used in certain situations.

<<copy>> is used to copy a requirement in read-only mode, <<trace>> being too generic. Can this concept be reserved for a later characterization not yet defined?

These links make it possible to ensure traceability between the levels, for most of the modeling elements and in a transverse way.

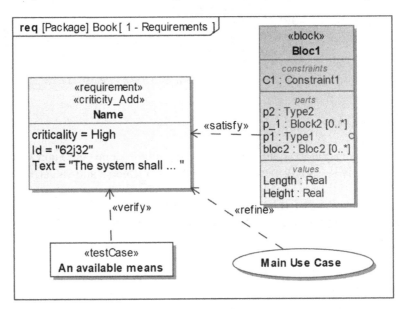

Figure 1.14. *Main traceability links*

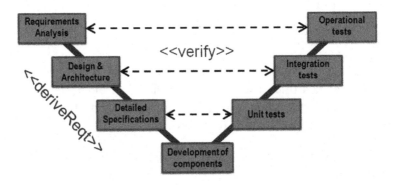

Figure 1.15. *V cycle: Traceability links*

1.11.6. *ReqIF*

The ReqIF (Requirement Interchange Format) is an international standard based on the XML format and adopted by the OMG as a formal specification for exchange of requirements between the software tools of different publishers.

You can find more details on this format on the OMG website: http://www.omg.org/spec/ReqIF/

Requirements
.Interchange Format

Figure 1.16. *Official OMG ReqIF logo*

Refer to section 4.2.1.1, particularly for importing requirements into a SysML model.

1.12. Use case diagram (uc)

This diagram is mainly used during the analysis phase in order to formalize and structure the macroscopic needs. It is composed of actors interacting with the system and use cases. These use cases will then be detailed in the form of scenarios.

The purpose of this diagram is to provide an overview of the functionalities provided to the actors, the objectives (represented in the form of use cases) and the possible dependencies between these use cases.

1.12.1. *Actor*

An actor defines a role endorsed either by a user or by any other system interacting with the system.

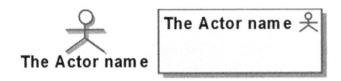

Figure 1.17. *Representations of an actor*

SysML provides different representations of actors, the best known being the stickman, see Figure 1.17. A possible variant being a rectangular representation, where the stickman appears as an icon. A tool like Cameo makes it possible to substitute an image for this representation,

1.12.2. *Use case*

A use case defines a major objective for an actor of the system and constitutes a set of actions executed by the system providing an observable result that is typically important for one or more actors or even other stakeholders in the system.

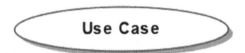

Figure 1.18. *Representation of a use case*

1.12.3. *Relations*

There are several relations between actor and use cases:

– communication: Connection between actors and use cases by an association;

– extension: Provides optional, non-mandatory features;

– inclusion: Factoring common features shared by several cases;

– generalization : provides varying management mechanisms, by inheritance.

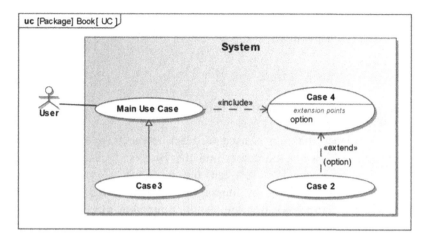

Figure 1.19. *Examples of relations between use cases*

Example of a textual format according to Alister Cockburn, the lines in italics are optional:

– use case: (use case name);

– actor: (main actor(s), triggers of the case);

– *event trigger*;

– stakeholders and their interests: (in list form);

– level: (Strategic, User Objective, or Sub-Functionality);

– scope: (Delimit the case scope);

– *pre-conditions: (Requirements for the case to be applicable)*;

– *post-conditions: (Consequences of successful application of the system)*;

– nominal Scenario: (List of different actions upon success of the system);

– *extensions: (List of all scenarios different from the nominal, followed by their conditions of realization as well as their actions and possibly use sub-cases)*;

– *constraints: (e.g. confidentiality, reactivity of actors...)*;

– open questions: (Allow the case to be improved by targeting the grey areas of the project);

– appendices.

1.13. The sequence diagram (sd)

The sequence diagram is used to describe the flow of exchanges (interactions) between the actors and the Blocks; it also allows the description of exchanges between the parts of a system. These exchanges are represented by messages transmitted and received by these entities, symbolized by lifelines; the time takes place along these vertical axes. A message is a unidirectional communication element between lines that triggers an activity in the recipient. Receiving a message causes an event at the receiver. The dashed arrow represents a return. This means that the message in question is the direct result of the previous message. A synchronous message (transmitter blocked waiting for response) is represented by a solid arrow, while an asynchronous message is represented by a hollow arrow.

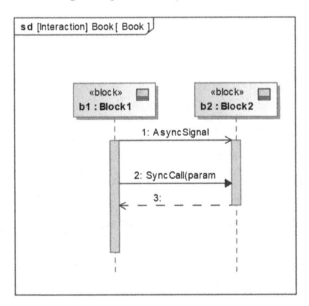

Figure 1.20. *Sequence diagram. For a color version of this figure, see www.iste.co.uk/casse/sysml.zip*

The arrow that loops (reflexive message or message to self) represents an internal behavior.

The vertical bands along a lifeline represent activation periods. They are optional, but allow a better understand of the dashed arrow of the return message.

1.13.1. *Lifeline*

A lifeline symbolizes an element participating in the interactions, serving as a basis for the exchanges in the form of messages, as well as the execution of a unit of behavior or local action. It is the vertical axis acting as a support for exchanges.

1.13.2. *Message*

This (unidirectional) communication element triggers an activity in the recipient by causing a local event. It may be synchronous, in this case represented by a solid arrow with the blocked transmitter awaiting a response, symbolized by a dotted line. It can be asynchronous, in which case the arrow is recessed in the transmitter block, see Figure 1.20 for these two message types. Finally it can be self-communicating (message to self), indicating the call of a local operation, either synchronously or asynchronously.

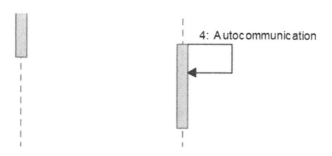

Figure 1.21. *Self-communicating message*

1.13.3. *Combined fragment*

This very precise notation allows the description of complex exchanges by specifying their scheduling, for example loops, parallelism, their optional character etc.

A fragment is used to group messages that are all dependent on this region, called an operand that has a guard (or condition) with the evaluation of a Boolean expression that is dependent on one and only one lifeline. If this expression returns a true result, the fragment will be executed. In Figure 1.22, [condition] will be evaluated.

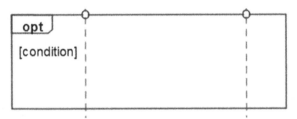

Figure 1.22. *Example of a combined fragment*

Here is the list of interaction operators:

1.13.3.1. *Alternatives (alt)*

Used to describe an alternative scenario, allowing if-then-else modeling.

1.13.3.2. *Assertion(assert)*

The sequences of this operand are the only valid continuations.

1.13.3.3. *Break*

Represents an interrupt-type scenario, executed instead of the rest of the fragment.

1.13.3.4. *Consider*

This means that only the local operand is considered, ignoring all other messages.

1.13.3.5. Critical

Allows you the definition of a critical region that cannot be interrupted by other occurrences on the lifelines covered by the region.

1.13.3.6. Ignore

Indication of non-significant messages that can be ignored, possibly occurring at any time in the sequence.

1.13.3.7. Loop

Allows the representation of a loop, with a minimum of iterations probably specified unless a constraint is deemed true.

1.13.3.8. Negative (neg)

Description by the negative of an invalid scenario.

1.13.3.9. Option (opt)

Describes an optional scenario, allowing if-then modeling.

1.13.3.10. Parallel (par)

Allows the representation of several scenarios executed in parallel, in other words, the order of execution is inconsistent.

1.13.3.11. Weak sequencing (seq)

Similar to the fragment except the events will be ordered in sequence.

1.13.3.12. Strict sequencing (strict)

Indicates a sequence that is strictly described, reinforcing the order.

1.13.4. Activity period (Execution)

The execution specification specifies the execution of a unit of behavior or local action on a lifeline, and therefore on the referenced element, in particular a block. Also called control or activation bar.

Figure 1.23. *Activity period*

1.13.5. *Invariant state*

An invariant state is an execution constraint for the participants in the interaction. It is modeled using the values of a property or a parameter, or a state (of a state machine) in which the lifeline must be located.

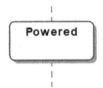

Figure 1.24. *Invariant state*

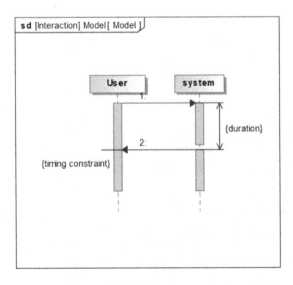

Figure 1.25. *Time management*

1.13.6. *Time*

The time progresses vertically from top to bottom and can be indicated as reference in the form of absolute time or delay. Moreover, it is possible to specify time or duration constraints, with a precise time or a range between brackets.

1.14. The package diagram (pkg)

The concept of a package is similar to that of a folder or directory for an operating system. It allows the modeling elements to be grouped according to a specific approach or simply by grouping them by family. Similarly, most SysML tools use the package as an exchange structure for importing and exporting model subsets. This is done in order to fulfill several objectives: reusability in the first place (from one project to another), then sharing between the different stakeholders of a project (update exchanges).

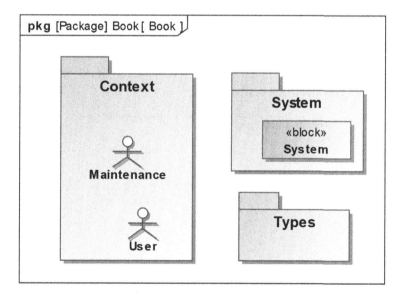

Figure 1.26. *Package diagram*

The pkg makes it possible to document the arrangement of the different elements, this architecture reflecting the recommendations from the approach or methodology implemented.

Good practice involves grouping together types and other shared definitions so as to facilitate their reuse and updating.

The SysML profile is thus stored by the tool separately from the rest of the model and is generally hidden, since the lambda user does not need to access its elements except to customize certain attributes; however, copying these elements in a dedicated profile is recommended to facilitate maintenance. Profiling for the domain is often necessary, but even although we do not fully address this in this book, the concept of stereotyping is presented here, the stereotypes being grouped in this particular package.

1.15. The block definition diagram (bdd)

The bdd defines the attributes of the blocks and their relationships such as associations, generalization and dependencies. The attributes of the blocks will be represented as a compartment. These attributes are values, operations, constraints, parts and references. The ports of the blocks can also be specified.

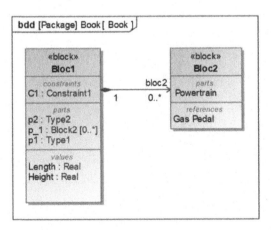

Figure 1.27. *The block definition diagram*

NOTE.– Why two diagrams for Blocks? In fact, regardless of the UML heritage, an explanatory comparison with a CAD tool is possible. Indeed, graphical design tools often offer symbol libraries (the bdd) to create schemas (the ibd). The bdd thus makes it possible to create this library (for the project) before the instantiation in an ibd. In absolute terms, a tool like CSM allowing the direct creation of Blocks in the repository, one could do without bdds and use only ibds, if only schematic views were necessary…

1.15.1. The block

Blocks are modular units of the system description. Each block defines a set of characteristics to describe a system or other interesting element. These can include both structural and behavioral characteristics, such as properties and operations, to represent the system state and behavior. The blocks have a generic capability for modeling systems into modular tree components. The specific types of components, the types of connections between them and how these elements combine to define the whole system can all be chosen according to the objectives of a specific system model. SysML blocks can be used in all system specification and design phases and can be applied to many types of systems. This includes modeling the logical or physical decomposition of a system, as well as the specifications of any software, hardware or human element. The components of these systems can interact by many different means, such as software operations, discrete state transitions, input and output flows, or continuous interactions.

1.15.2. Properties

A block may have different properties: values, parts, or references.

These properties can be represented graphically and grouped into optional compartments. Other special properties are used, ports for specifying the allowable types of interaction between blocks and constraints specifying the constraints between other block properties.

1.15.3. *Values*

Values (value properties) are properties that can be described in a quantifiable way by a value type, possibly dependent on a domain with a dimension and a unit.

1.15.4. *Operations*

An operation describes the behavior of a block; it has a name, ending with brackets, a type, parameters (incoming, outgoing or bidirectional) and constraints.

Any operation can be called by an action that sends a request to a target element, in which the requested behavior is executed. This request may be synchronous or asynchronous.

1.15.5. *Constraints*

This involves a mechanism for integrating technical analyses from performance or reliability models. A constraint is usually expressed mathematically as an equation that constrains the physical properties of a system.

1.15.6. *Ports*

The port is a connection point on which external elements can connect and interact in a different or restrictive way unlike a direct connection. Ports are Block properties and define the functionality accessible by external elements via connectors between ports. These features can be properties, including flow properties, associations, operations and receiving. A flow property specifies what can be exchanged between blocks; it can be data, energy, matter (solid, liquid or gas), while the flow elements indicate what is actually exchanged by the connectors. (Refer to Chapter 2 on the internal block diagram).

NOTE.– The direction that is displayed on the port is actually the combination of the flow properties' directions belonging to the block typing the port. If the block typing the port does not have stream properties, there is no arrow on the port symbol. If the direction of all flow properties is "in", the port will have the incoming arrow on its symbol. If the direction of all the flow properties is "out", the port will have the outgoing arrow. Otherwise, the port will have a two-way arrow on its symbol. If the port is set to be conjugated, the arrow will be reversed.

1.15.7. Associations

An association represents the link between blocks. There are several types of associations: reference, composite and shared.

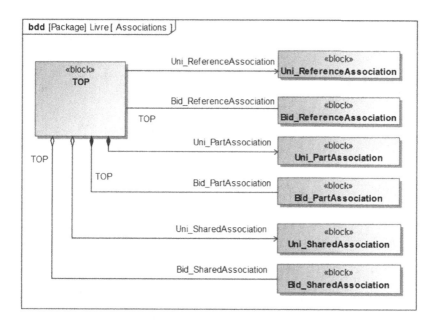

Figure 1.28. *Example of associations*

1.15.7.1. *Multiplicity*

Multiplicity, also called cardinality, specifies the number of instances an element at one end of an association can have.

Possible values are 1, *, 0..*, 0..n, n, n..n (n being any positive integer), meaning one, several, none to many, none to n, n, from n to n, respectively.

1.15.7.2. *Role*

Each of the ends of an association can be named to indicate the role of the elements connected by this association. Just like in most diagrams, it is possible to represent a relation by "lines and arrows", or by compartment. In Figure 1.29, there is strict equivalence between the top and bottom.

By creating the top diagram, dragging and dropping blocks into a new diagram will automatically reveal the compartments, with the roles and the associated blocks, the notion of reference is explained later.

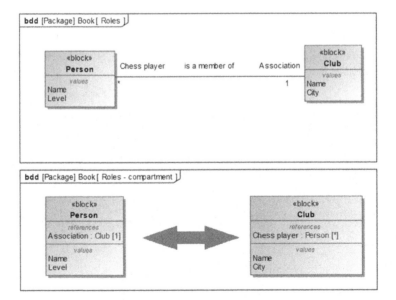

Figure 1.29. *Roles and equivalent representations*

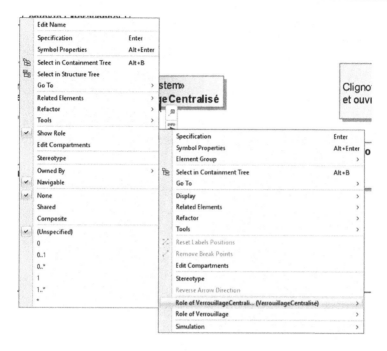

Figure 1.30. *Affectation of roles*

1.15.8. *Reference*

This is the simplest of associations, of the type equal to equal.

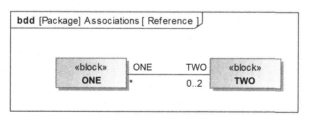

Figure 1.31. *Association without aggregation*

Be careful not to confuse the name of this association with the property of a Block whose objective is to mention the elements connected by a non-composite association.

1.15.9. *Composite*

This represents the parts of a Block, in other words the other Blocks that compose it. If the encompassing Block is destroyed, its parts will also be destroyed. The term composition (or strong aggregation) is also used.

The multiplicity of the composite side (the black diamond) can only be 1 or 0.1, indeed a part can, by definition, only belong to one composite at a time.

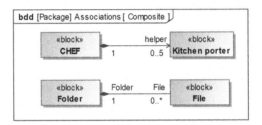

Figure 1.32. *Composite association*

1.15.10. *Shared*

Unlike parts, if the Block containing these components is destroyed, the components will not be eliminated in turn. They are therefore more independently part of the system. The term aggregation is also used.

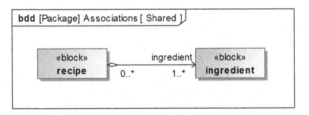

Figure 1.33. *Shared association*

1.15.11. *Generalization*

The opposite of specialization, this is a key concept to propagate the properties of an element (here a block) to its "children" by inheritance. The strong idea is to factorize common properties for several blocks with strong similarities, yet with some unique features additional to those already shared. If the parent block is not used directly in the model, it will be called an abstract block.

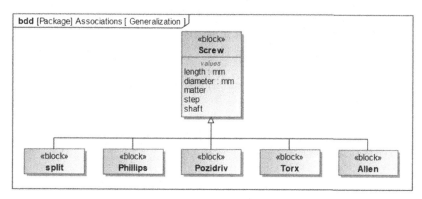

Figure 1.34. *Generalization and specialization*

1.15.12. *Dependency*

This is a type of relationship for which one or more elements require other elements for their specification or implementation. There is therefore a dependence on the source element. This relationship is not used much for Blocks, the notion of use is an example, but we will come back to this when we discuss the requirements. Indeed, in this diagram there are a large number of dependencies: derivation, satisfaction, conformity, realization, refinement, allocation, copy, verification etc.

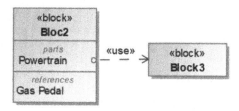

Figure 1.35. *Use dependency*

1.15.13. *Direction*

Some associations may be either bidirectional or unidirectional. To indicate a single direction, an arrow will indicate the direction of that association.

When an association is unidirectional, the target side (the arrow side) does not reference the source.

Usually unidirectional (Directed) associations are used.

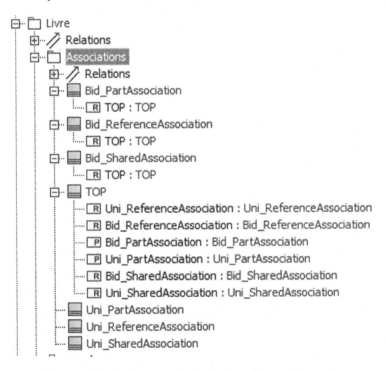

Figure 1.36. *Reference of associations. For a color version of this figure, see www.iste.co.uk/casse/sysml.zip*

NOTE.– Here the Blocks prefixed by 'Uni' do not contain a reference to the TOP Block to which they are linked, unlike the Blocks prefixed by 'Bid' which contain a reference to the TOP Block.

1.15.14. *Compartments*

It is possible to represent all the properties of a Block in the form of compartments. However, for associations, it is not possible to mix the representation of compartment and their graphical equivalence (lines and symbols). In other words, the choice will be exclusive for the same diagram, since it is possible to choose per diagram the information to be represented.

Below is the compartment representation equivalent to Figure 1.28.

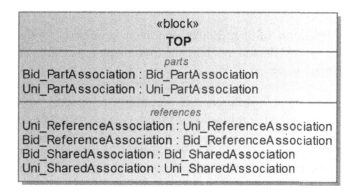

Figure 1.37. *Example of compartments*

1.16. The internal block diagram (ibd)

The ibd defines the internal structure of a block and its properties as well as the connectors linking these properties. This diagram is much more useful for the communication of the system specifications than the block definition diagram, which can be used for the creation of blocks, and in particular their properties. Indeed the ibd is very relevant for many trades, as it is comparable to a diagram. Here, we will use the connectors, linked to the ports of the parts and references to do this.

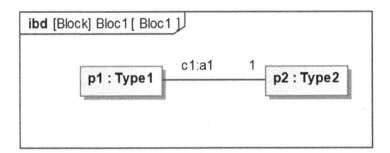

Figure 1.38. *Internal block diagram*

The definition of the Blocks and their properties having been discussed in the chapter on bdd; in this chapter we will study the particularities of an ibd.

The most notable difference is the ability to specify what flows between ports, whether it is a flow of fluid, energy, matter or data.

In other words, in a bdd it is possible to specify the associations between Blocks and generalisation links, but in no case what they exchange.

NOTE.– Why two diagrams for Blocks? Here is a second explanation additional to that provided in the note in section 1.15. For those who have already used a programming language like the C language, a bdd would be comparable to the prototyping of a function, whereas an ibd would approximately correspond to the body of this function.

1.16.1. *Connectors*

In an ibd, we will no longer directly use Blocks, but instead, the parts or instantiated references from them. The ibd will then form, contextually, a representation of the connections. These connections are called connectors. All these properties and connectors belong to the Block on which the ibd depends. This Block is the context of the ibd. Connectors can connect parts or references directly to each other, or connect them via ports.

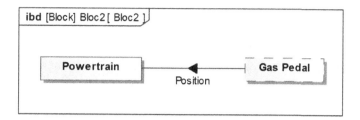

Figure 1.39. *Connector without port*

1.16.2. *Ports*

We will consider the most recent definitions supported by SysML 1.5, using two types of ports: Active or Complete <<full>> and Passive or Auxiliary <<proxy>>.

SysML allows the possibility of not typing the ports at the beginning, in order to reserve the choice of the type for a later phase.

NOTE.– CSM indicates a "simple" port (neither <<full>>, nor <<proxy>>) by a green color for the outline and beige for the background.

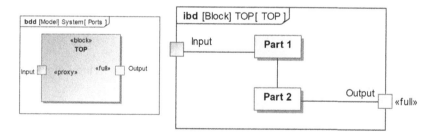

Figure 1.40. *Example of ports. For a color version of this figure, see www.iste.co.uk/casse/sysml.zip*

In this example, we created two ports, one input and one output, on the TOP Block at the bdd. This Block is represented in the form of a black box, although it is possible to specify its composition in parts, as seen previously. Then, in order to develop the structure of this block into a white box, we create an ibd.

By creating this ibd, we see that the ports appear at the edges of our ibd diagram, on the frame, to indicate that they are interfaces between the TOP block (or its parts). We can refine later on what is exchanged between these parts, through which ports these data, fluids, energy and matter pass, and their type etc.

1.16.3. *Full*

This type of port is considered separate from the block containing it, and can be viewed as one of its parts.

This port is typed by a block and can therefore represent a complex entity.

The indication of this type of port is reinforced by the use of the stereotype <<full>>.

NOTE.– CSM highlights the type of port <<full>> with a beige color (background and outline).

1.16.4. *Proxy*

This type of port allows you to reveal properties of a block to other blocks.

Unlike the Full Port it does not describe a separate element of the block nor its parts.

This port can be typed only by an Interface Block; like any other typing, this must be done at the bdd level.

The indication of this type of port is reinforced by the use of the <<proxy>> stereotype.

NOTE.– CSM highlights the <<proxy>> port in a green color (background and outline).

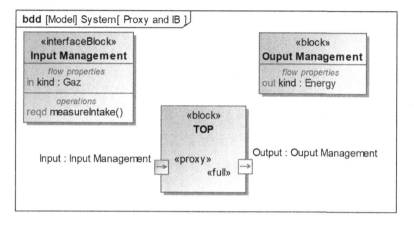

Figure 1.41. *Proxy port and its typing by interface Blocks*

1.16.5. *Interface Blocks*

This block is specific to the typing of passive <<proxy>> ports.

It has neither a behavior nor parts, but it has, in principle, a set of flow properties that can be displayed in a dedicated compartment.

See the previous figure (Figure 1.41), in which the interface block Input Management types the Input port, which is of type <<proxy>>. This is an interesting use of the bdd to document the characterization of ports.

1.16.6. *Flow elements/Property*

The item property is the only characteristic of flow elements.

A flow element describes the flow of elements through a connector or an association. It is most often found in an ibd on connectors.

Each element will have a meaning, from the source to the destination.

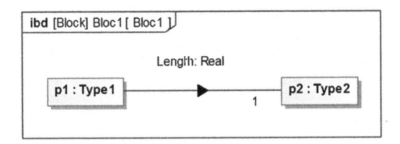

Figure 1.42. *A flow element*

NOTE.– The direction that is displayed on the port is actually a combination of the directions of the flow properties belonging to the block typing the port. If the block typing the port does not have flow properties, there is no arrow on the port symbol. If the direction of all flow properties is "in", the port will have the incoming arrow on its symbol. If the direction of all the flow properties is "out", the port will have the outgoing arrow. Otherwise, the port will have a two-way arrow on its symbol. If the port is set to be conjugated, the arrow will be reversed.

1.17. The parametric diagram (par)

The par makes it possible to integrate into the model, representations of constraints or equations for analysis. Measurements of performance and efficiency can be provided.

Each constraint is first defined by parameters as well as a rule describing the evolution of the parameters with respect to one another. A constraint is represented by a block with a <<constraint>> stereotype. This diagram is defined as a limited form of the ibd, a kind of specialization. The specification language of the constraints is informal; nevertheless, it is possible to use a more formal language such as OCL or even MathML, Modelica etc.

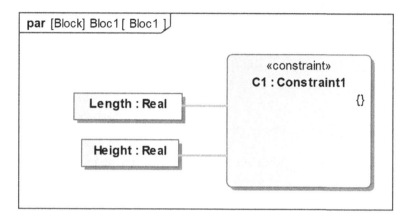

Figure 1.43. *Parametric diagram*

1.17.1. *Constraint*

SysML provides in the form of a block property the possibility of expressing a constraint, shown in brackets, in a dedicated compartment (see section 1.15.14). The parametric diagram makes it possible to represent these constraints graphically. To do this, there is a dedicated Block type, the constraint Block.

Besides constraints, this block contains a set of typed parameters.

In other words, we define the parameters of the equations by this type of Block, which are called constraints in SysML.

1.17.2. *Binding connector*

This is the only type of connector allowed. At least one end must be connected to a constraint parameter.

The properties of each end must have equal values, implying that their type is identical, or that it is compatible.

1.17.3. *Value binding*

This is how to maintain equivalent values of properties that are linked together. The binding connector is used to represent this connection, with respect to the compatibility of the typing.

1.18. The state machine diagram (stm)

This diagram is based on the diagram invented by David Harel himself taking the well-known concept of the finite state machine, with a number of extensions such as the encapsulation of states (Russian dolls) in composite states, or Pseudo-states (default, history etc.). This diagram is attached to a Block to describe its behavior. If this Block is of type <<system>> then the state machine is used to describe the system modes.

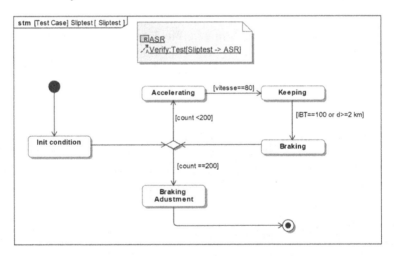

Figure 1.44. *State machine diagram*

1.18.1. *State*

A state represents a life phase of a block, this phase having a certain stability.

The simplest category, the atomic state, can have three regions: entry, do (ultimately decomposed) and exit. These regions are a good way to optimize (by factoring) the number of transitions and also to improve readability. With regard to the region do/activity, the latter, even if it is continuous, will be interrupted as soon as it leaves the state which supports it.

Figure 1.45. *Atomic state*

The composite state is a unique category, which allows the encapsulation of states (like Russian dolls) in order to powerfully factorize certain states or transitions.

Finally, the notion of orthogonal state, decomposed into several regions, is available, but it somewhat contradicts our approach so we will not be using it.

1.18.2. *Composite states*

Composite states (or super-states) are used to represent a decomposition into sub-reports in order to detail the behavior. It is possible to transfer this decomposition to another lower level diagram in order to dissimilate it, usually so as not to overload the graphic. A chain symbol may appear to represent this. The figure below, (Figure 1.46) is the transformation of Figure 1.51, which you will find further down.

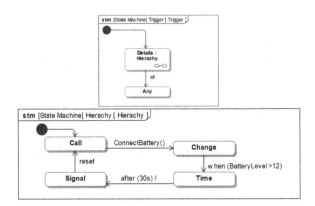

Figure 1.46. *Composite state with sub machine*

1.18.3. *Parallel states*

A state can be decomposed into several regions, separated by dotted lines, in order to represent competing behaviors or parallel executions.

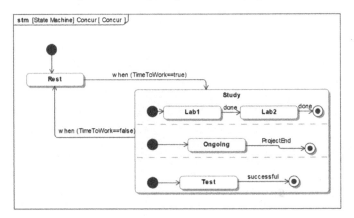

Figure 1.47. *Orthogonal state and its regions*

We will not use this option (by methodological choice); nevertheless it is good to know this option, though it is unfortunately misused too often. This technique is not very elegant and even displays a bad functional analysis; we therefore very strongly discourage this!

1.18.4. *Pseudo-states*

These are more connectors than states; the system is not supposed to spend time in them. We will not discuss the following pseudo states: Entry, Terminate, Exit, Fork, Join, Choice and Junction; however, they are illustrated in the figure below (Figure 1.48).

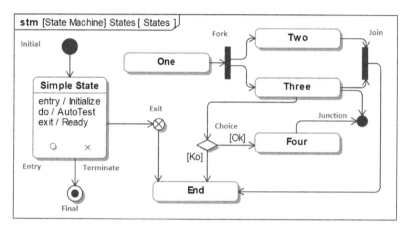

Figure 1.48. *Pseudo-states. For a color version of this figure, see www.iste.co.uk/casse/sysml.zip*

1.18.4.1. *Initial*

This is the only mandatory pseudo-state, since it indicates the starting point of the automaton. In Figure 1.44, the connection state is "initial condition".

Watch out for the Junction connector that resembles it in every way...

1.18.4.2. *Final*

Optional, this means to stop the execution of the active level, or even the complete automaton.

1.18.4.3. *History*

This is available in two versions: Shallow and Deep.

A H appears in this pseudo-state, and Deep has an asterisk on the top right of the symbol to distinguish it from Shallow, which does not.

This mechanism allows a back-up of the state configuration; in other words, it indicates a memorization of the last visited state of a composite state, the last time a transition exited, regardless of the transitions leading to it. This mechanism is thus very convenient as it avoids the need to model a recording of the context and then its restoration.

1.18.5. *Transition*

A transition allows the transition from one state to another. It is symbolized by a solid line with an arrow at its end, of a unique type, unlike the Flows of the activity diagram. It is triggered by a trigger ultimately associated with a guard or condition and can perform an activity of various types, particularly actions. These actions can be atomic or complex, and correspond to the transmission or receipt of a trigger.

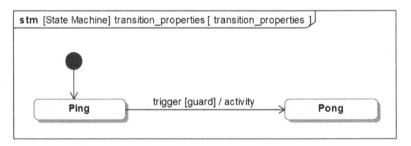

Figure 1.49. *Set of properties of a transition*

There is the possibility of defining an internal transition, named as such because, as for the entry, do and exit regions, it appears to be a compartment and is characterized by a purely local execution; the other regions are not executed, since we do not enter or exit the state. It is possible to use a state as source and target at the same time; this transition is then known as reflexive (or self-triggering).

1.18.6. *Trigger events*

There are many types, typed by modeling or even automatically generated.

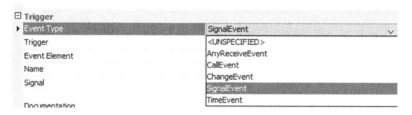

Figure 1.50. *Types of triggers*

The figure above (Figure 1.50) illustrates the choice of event, and the figure below (Figure 1.51) represents an example of representation:

– "reset" represents a signal;

– "Connect Battery" represents an operation call;

– "when" (BatteryLevel > 12) represents a change of values;

– "after" (30s) represents a time delay;

– "all" represents a trigger by any signal.

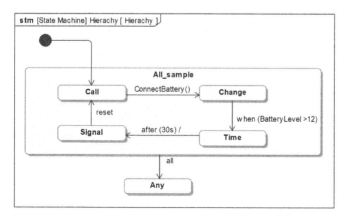

Figure 1.51. *Examples of triggers*

1.18.6.1. *SignalEvent*

The default and simplest event, the SignalEvent represents the receipt of an instance of an asynchronous signal AnyReceiveEvent.

1.18.6.2. *AnyReceiveEvent*

The type AnyReceiveEvent is global to all messages, the keyword "all" is used in this case.

1.18.6.3. *CallEvent*

The CallEvent type is triggered on receipt of an instance of a message requiring an operation.

NOTE.– The brackets are characteristic of an operation. e.g. LaunchDiagnostic().

1.18.6.4. *ChangeEvent*

This allows the result of a Boolean expression to be transformed when it is true in a trigger. The keyword "when" is used.

1.18.6.5. *TimeEvent*

At a specified time, a signal is triggered, i.e. a timer is set and when it is over, the trigger is activated.

The time can be relative, with the use of the keyword "after" or the time can be absolute (by dating) with the use of the keyword "at()".

1.18.7. *Guard*

Labeled in brackets, the guard condition is a Boolean expression used to validate the execution of the transition when its value is true. See the description of action language below, since the same comments are given for the semantics, in particular for the set of Boolean and relational operators that can be used.

NOTE.– In order to avoid the indeterminisms that could occur when several transitions are executed simultaneously, the keyword "else" can be used.

1.18.8. *Activity and Action Language*

SysML does not specifically represent semantics for the language corresponding to the activity triggered by a transition (also called effect or action). This gives the editor of the modeling tool a lot of freedom to implement the model in order to perform a simulation, or any other analysis, of the model properties.

As shown in the following figure, Cameo proposes to associate:

– an activity (a diagram which combines a series of actions);

– an interaction diagram (the sequence diagram);

– another state machine;

– "opaque" behavior, meaning that its description is not derived from the SysML toolkit, typically from the computer programming language;

– or functional behavior (which is a subset of the opaque form) limited to the transformation of input values into output values without any other impact on the rest of the system.

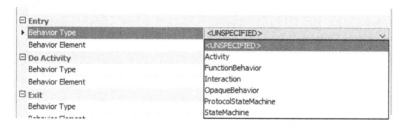

Figure 1.52. *Types of behaviors proposed by Cameo*

NOTE.– The ProtocolStateMachine behavior type comes from Cameo's UML inheritance, normally not available in SysML.

Different languages are available for the description of the behavior, the natural language being proposed by default. Executable languages are available, such as MATLAB, OCL, JavaScript or even a proprietary approach built into Cameo that can be used by a built-in solver (Built-in Math).

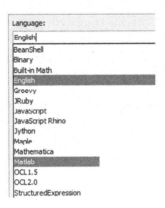

Figure 1.53. *Available action languages*

1.19. The activity diagram (act)

This diagram combines actions/functions, the notion of linking in time and the data exchanged is extremely rich. In particular, it allows the use of an EFFBD (Enhanced Function Flow Block Diagram) or other formalizations.

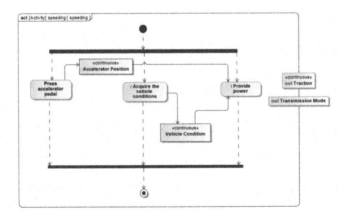

Figure 1.54. *Activity Diagram*

Modeling system activity increases the coordination of block-dependent behaviors by inputs, outputs, sequences and conditions. In other words, it is a flexible link to the behavior of blocks. An activity consists of a series of actions which are linked either by a control flow or by an exchange (object) or data flow.

Note that an activity can be defined in a bdd in the form of a block (which is the way to type in SysML) with the keyword "activity".

1.19.1. *Action*

This is a fundamental execution element that represents a transformation or processing in the system being modeled. An action can be discrete or continuous.

In the above figure, "Press accelerator" is an action.

Special types of action, allowing synchronization of an activity upon receipt of a trigger, the trigger of a timer or the sending of a signal, are available.

Cameo offers a vast number of tools: two particularly interesting ones are Call Operation and Call Behavior. This allows you to instantiate other activities.

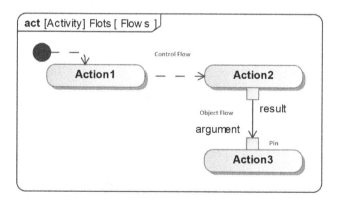

Figure 1.55. *Representation of two types of flow and pin. For a color version of this figure, see www.iste.co.uk/casse/sysml.zip*

1.19.2. *Control flow*

Represented by a dotted line (convention) terminated by an arrow, the flow simply indicates the sequence of actions. This sequence may be specified by decision, fusion, fork or junction nodes.

1.19.3. *Exchange Flow (or Object Flow)*

An Object Flow is represented by a continuous line (convention) terminated by an arrow; this flow (connected to pins located on the actions) also indicates the order of linkage in order to specify what is consumed, produced or processed by an action.

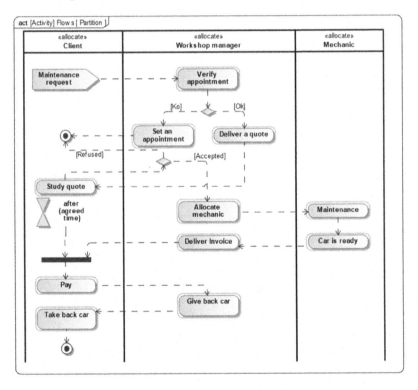

Figure 1.56. *Example of allocation by partition*

1.19.4. *Pin*

A pin may have an input or output direction that is compatible with the direction of the object flow to which it is connected.

1.19.5. *Partition*

We will approach this concept during transverse modeling as it allows the graphical representation of an allocation of actions to other elements.

The term swim lane is also used instead of partition (SwimLane).

1.19.6. *Event Receipt*

This particular action (AcceptEvent) is waiting for an event generated outside of the activity. In Figure 1.57 below, "RESET" is an example of this.

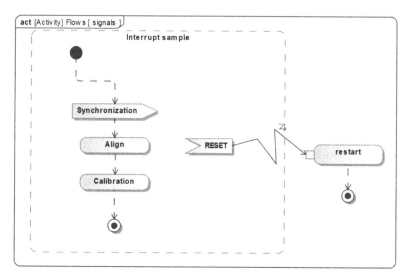

Figure 1.57. *Example of handling an exception*

1.19.7. *Signal transmission*

This action (SendSignal) sends a signal to a target capable of processing this signal.

In Figure 1.57 above, "Synchronisation" is an example of this.

1.19.8. *Interruptible Region*

The particular use case of the receipt of a signal where a flow linked to this region will allow the overall interruption of the executed actions located in this region. The previous figure (Figure 1.57) illustrates this mechanism.

1.19.9. *Time Delay*

Represented as an hourglass, a timer will generate a time-related system event. As with state diagrams, the time can be absolute, "at()", or relative, "after()".

In Figure 1.56 above, "at (Convenient Time)" is an example of this.

1.20. View and view point

The concepts of view and view point are described by the standard ISO-42010 (formerly IEEE-1471) with which SysML is in line.

1.20.1. *View*

A view shows a specific perspective using a particular package. Examples include operational, manufacturing and safety perspectives.

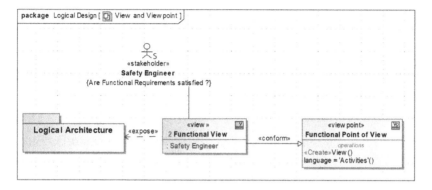

Figure 1.58. *A view point example*

1.20.2. *View point*

A view point is the specification of the content of a view, composed of convention and rules allowing the construction and use of this view. Typically a view point contains diagrams. The objective in SysML is to allow the description of the stakeholder expectations by structuring the artifacts that are useful for better understanding.

1.21. List of SysML keywords

It may be wise to avoid the use of these keywords in order to minimize any ambiguity or even conflict in the use of models as well as of tools.

Of course, some of these words are very common, so precaution should be taken mainly where these keywords might be present, typically in behavioral diagrams (stm, act and sd); for the relations between and with the requirements, these keywords usually appear as a stereotype (e.g. <<verify>> or even <<satisfy>>), which limits the risk of ambiguity.

at, all, after, when, do, opt, operation, allocation, alt and else are some examples; refer to the glossary to identify others.

1.22. For more information

There are many pages on the OMG website where you can find more details; here are some examples of useful links:

– http://www.omgsysml.org/index.htm;

– http://www.omg.org/spec/SysML/;

– http://www.omgsysml.org/INCOSE-OMGSysML-Tutorial-Final-090901.pdf.

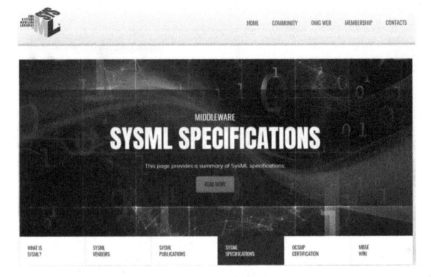

Figure 1.59. *Official site about SysML. For a color version of this figure, see www.iste.co.uk/casse/sysml.zip*

1.23. Common elements

SysML offers some elements and relationships common to all diagrams. In particular, Note and Comment. For comments, two variants, <<problem>> and <<rational>>, are proposed in order to specify the nature of a problem to be solved or even the textual justification of the presence of an element. A grapnel symbolizing the attachment to the elements is available in all cases.

NOTE.– Note the difference between a note and a comment (also valid for the variants <<problem>> and <<rational>>) is important. A note is only present graphically and locally on a diagram (without a link to the model), whereas comments are elements of models, thus present in the repository and reusable. Comments can have compartments and be stereotyped (e.g. <<AttachedFile>> to create a link to an external file). A double click will open this file, for example a text file (PDF, Word) or image, spreadsheet, etc.

2

About Cameo Systems Modeler

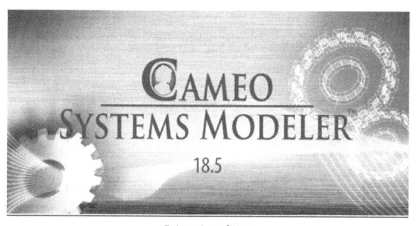

Figure 2.1. *Cameo Systems Modeler start-up screen. For a color version of this figure, see www.iste.co.uk/casse/sysml.zip*

2.1. Overview of Cameo Systems Modeler

Cameo Systems Modeler, which we will call CSM or Cameo, is currently one of the flagship tools for modeling complex systems based on a collaborative environment. I find it very intuitive, robust and possibly the tool with one of the best compatibilities with the standard System Modeling Language (SysML). In addition, it has import/export capabilities like other SysML tools on the market, thus guaranteeing a certain durability. Other interfaces are presented in the framework of interoperability to other tools (requirement management via ReqIF or API format, csv type office files, PLM, CAD, mathematical simulation, embedded systems etc.). CSM is available on many platforms such as MS Windows, UNIX (Linux, Mac etc.) including as a portable version, requiring no installation.

A modeling tool like CSM is developed to offer system engineers an efficient way to create SysML models and also to be part of a more global Model-Based System Engineering (MBSE) approach; of course, other tools are necessary in order to ensure the entire engineering process is covered.

CSM has many additional modules (or plug-ins), some requiring a purchase, others available free of charge. The main plug-ins extend the capabilities of the tool such as simulation, remote model sharing, product line management, variants etc. Some plug-ins allow CSM to be integrated into an existing tool chain, supporting interoperability with third-party tools, as illustrated in the following table mentioning the CSM ecosystem. Other plug-ins are additional profiles or examples, templates etc.

We will not list these modules (which are frequently developing); however, some will be used in our case study to illustrate advanced uses. Refer to Chapter 5.

NOTE.– Cameo Systems Modeler is one of the versions of the historical tool MagicDraw. MagicDraw offers a large number of profiles to specialize in the use of certain features. CSM is specifically designed for an MBSE approach, with customizable menus to hide the UML-related part. There is no difference in the use of CSM or

MagicDraw with the SysML profile. CSM includes, in addition to editors and the SysML profile, simulation.

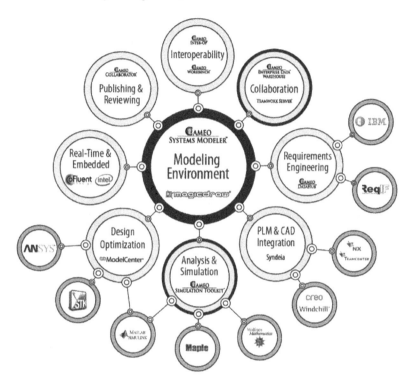

Figure 2.2. *Cameo Systems Modeler Ecosystem. For a color version of this figure, see www.iste.co.uk/casse/sysml.zip*

As mentioned above, SysML is a pivot language capable of expressing a large number of System Engineering concepts. However, many disciplines are not directly or completely covered. In addition, some professions in which SysML is applied probably use tools, the majority are more specialized and known as "business" tools, based on other languages, with more analytical, design, simulation or testing capabilities since they usually cover a more specific area of expertise. It is then necessary to ensure interoperability with these tools.

2.2. Installation

This part will not be discussed; however, we have used the default installation options, validated on multiple machines in a Windows environment. However, some customization settings are available below.

When writing this book, the current version of Cameo Systems Modeler was Version 18.5.

CSM V18.5 includes the modeler, the core solution, the SysML profile (compatible with SysML Version 1.4) and the simulation module.

NOTE.– A portable version is available, making it easier to maintain the tool, or alternatively using several different versions simultaneously, not obliging all stakeholders to use the latest version (which is still recommended). The compatibility of the license is still to be verified.

2.3. Availability of the model

The finalized model, where you can navigate from the content chart, will be available for free download and on request from the author: olivier.casse.consulting@gmail.com.

NOTE.– A free version of MagicDraw is available; although the models cannot be saved, existing projects can be opened in read-only mode. It is the "reader" version that to which one can add the SysML profile in order to transform it into CSM "reader" (No simulation).

Several videos showing the different stages and demonstrating a simulation scenario can also be viewed on the No Magic YouTube channel.

Finally, a HTML version of the documentation generated from CSM will be available online, allowing navigation in the model, to see its composition as well as the attributes of the different elements without needing to install CSM.

2.4. Covered tool features

We will not go through all the features of CSM, but instead look at the modeling techniques. No Magic offers several tutorials, in document format, accessible from the menu.

Several videos are also available on the website or the No Magic blog, including the basic principles of editing, shortcuts. It is recommended that you become familiar with these specificities; the time you devote to it will largely pay off in your first business project.

2.4.1. The Cameo simulation toolkit

This is a set of features grouped together to enable validation and verification of the system's dynamic aspects.

These include co-simulation, where CSM interacts with a third-party tool (MATLAB/Simulink, Maple, Modelica and fmus modules), compromise evaluation, model testing (discussed below) or even a verification of requirements in tabular form.

NOTE.– An fmu (Functional Mock-up Unit) module is a simulation model or library that implements the standard FMI (Functional Mock-up Interface). For more information, see: www.fmi-standard.org.

This is all driven by a traditional debugging interface, which means that it can be found in most model or code debugging tools.

The control interface of the simulation includes the start, stop, pause, activation/deactivation of the automatic animation (with the opening of the current diagram), access to variables (including triggers), break points and finally a console for entering manual commands (with choice of the action language) and collecting a four-level execution trace (Info, Debug, Error and Warning).

The ability to integrate interface prototyping panels with the user is an undeniable asset. In the final chapter, some practical cases of these features in our example will be illustrated, since they are truly essential to a consistent MBSE approach.

Finally, CSM can be used as a powerful Model Based Testing (MBT) tool because some diagrams can be executed as stimuli, or to compare the results obtained (verdicts).

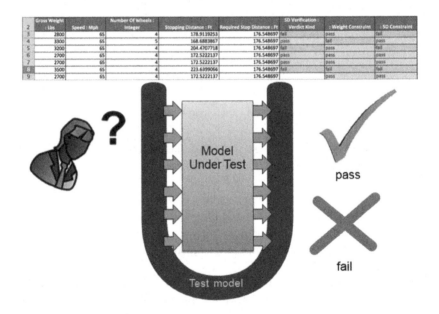

Figure 2.3. *Test automation. For a color version of this figure, see www.iste.co.uk/casse/sysml.zip*

2.4.2. *Documentation, user support and examples*

The documentation is fairly traditional in Acrobat Reader pdf format. It includes several documents: user guides, tutorials, for the main modeling tool as well as its options. Online help is also available by pressing the F1 key (Windows PC) in a conventional way; however, an online version (internet connection required) is available, with advantages such as more frequent updates and improved navigability.

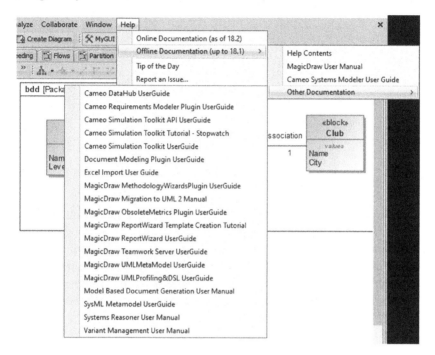

Figure 2.4. *Access to CSM documentation on and offline*

NOTE.– There are two versions of documentation, one available on-ine, the most up-to-date, and one available offline, installed with CSM.

The online version is navigable in HTML format, with a rather elaborate search mode, especially for SysML, with examples and links.

A very large number of examples are proposed; these examples are accessible from the tool home page and classified by interest. It is recommended to browse through them to discover the different possibilities offered by the MBSE approach, the SysML language and the basic or advanced functionalities of CSM.

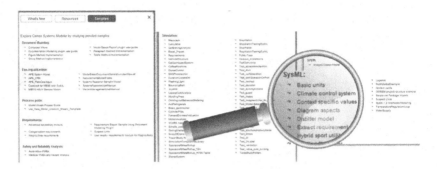

Figure 2.5. *List of examples*

2.4.3. *Setup*

There are some interesting options that significantly contribute to the MBSE approach, in particular simulation and document generation. The setup of CSM is very comprehensive, allowing customization to the modeling environment, but this setup requires experience in using the tool. It is advisable to scan all the options to familiarize yourself; during your first models, you will accumulate specific ergonomic needs.

It is also recommended to position the various options available in the menu according to your preferences. CSM offers a very large set of parameters; some can be very useful on a daily basis. Here is a brief overview:

– *Language*: English by default, the display language can be changed, for example to French, in the menu Option-Environment-General-Display.

– *Spelling*: Several dictionaries that spell check the text are available in the menu Option-Environment-General-Spelling. You can also add your own.

– *Last project*: Practical to automatically open the current project: Option-Environment-General-Save/Load, check Open Last project on Startup.

– *Expert Mode*: Option-Environment-Experience: Useful if you want to access all the menus and their commands, without going through the expert mode each time.

– *Role*: Options-Perspective-Customize: This is usually a user query; it is possible to customize the menus, assigning a particular role, the list of available options and commands will be customized.

NOTE.– For simulation, it is important for time management to specify the unit of time, if you express your timers in the form after (2) this will indicate a measurement of 2ms; after (2s) indicates a measurement of 2 seconds as CSM will understand.

We must consider several stages in the creation of our model, or more exactly several customizable categories. Indeed, upstream of the modeling itself we must take into account the implementation of the model, often sharing it, managing the different versions, interfacing with other tools etc.

In our case, I believe that you, the reader, will be working alone on the model, but I hope that during a subsequent use of your approach and the associated tools, these tips will be useful!

The fundamental aspect of modeling, whatever the language and tool used, is how to create (and destroy, see later on) the elements.

2.5. Creation of the project/structuring

2.5.1. *Packages*

Packages are used to define where to classify the various elements, tables and diagrams that make up the model (not to mention relationships).

A trick will be to use a numerical prefix so that the tool, which sorts the items alphanumerically by default, lists the packages in the order we are interested in, for example: (1) Operational Analysis, (2) System Requirements etc.

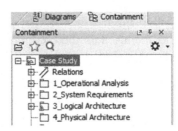

Figure 2.6. *Creation of the project structure via packages*

In each package, we will also create packages to group our items together to find them more easily.

For example, in the Operational Analysis package, User Requirements, subpackages, Context, Use cases, etc.

The documentation generated for our example will allow you to understand the chosen structure.

2.6. The content diagram

The use of the content diagram, usually with a background image on which the diagrams will be dragged/dropped, will create links to improve navigability.

CSM allows the use of a diagram specific to the tool, not from SysML, the content diagram. Its objective is to represent a project structure and thus constitutes a navigable table of contents. An image can be inserted as wallpaper to illustrate the procedure. Then you can overlay a shortcut to the diagrams, double-click to open them (to edit them or just view them), the diagrams in turn can include links to the table of contents or other diagrams.

Hyperlinks can also be created from any element of a diagram, for example from a use case to open the associated sequence diagram.

NOTE.– It is possible to associate several diagrams or elements according to the need, the tool then allows you to choose the one that you wish to open.

NOTE.– CSM provides a wizard to automatically create a content diagram from a set of diagrams.

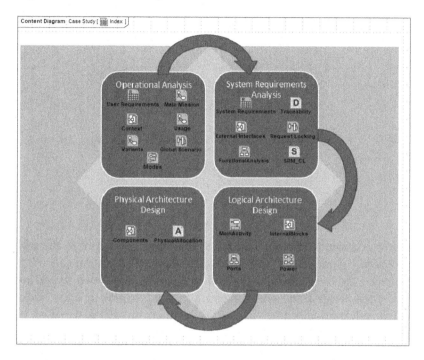

Figure 2.7. *Table of contents and navigation in the project. For a color version of this figure, see www.iste.co.uk/casse/sysml.zip*

In this diagram we have the index, with an image inserted serving as background to group links to the main diagrams, from the methodology, ensuring maximum navigability. This diagram should be visible from the project root.

It is possible to create a contextual content diagram at each level, detailing, for example, the links between the diagrams.

This also offers another possibility, not used in this example, which would be the insertion of images illustrating concepts other than SysML, bringing an additional aspect to the project. Similarly, it is possible to associate an external document using hyperlinks, for example, an Acrobat Reader PDF document.

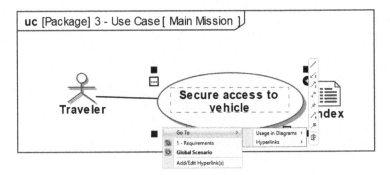

Figure 2.8. *Insertion of a link to navigate in the project*

In the example above (Figure 2.8), the option to return to the table of contents (Index) has been inserted. Note at the bottom left of the use case, the symbol indicates that on the use case, two hyperlinks have been created, the one appearing in bold will be opened with a double click on this use case. A right click on this symbol at the bottom left will open a hyperlink management menu.

2.7. Uniqueness of modeling elements

It seems appropriate now to specify that SysML modelers such as CSM rank all the elements making up the model (or set of models) in order to ensure their uniqueness in the repository. The diagrams are only a representation of the combination of a part of these elements in order to form specific points of view relevant to a particular category of readers.

In order to obtain an ideal modeling guide, it is recommended to drag and drop the majority of the elements from the repository (here the confinement tree) into the diagrams; however, certain constructions (relationships in particular) will be much more convenient to model in the diagrams.

In comparison, SysML elements correspond to words in a dictionary, where sentence writing would use these words in the same way that a model uses graphic objects that are only instances of the SysML elements present in the repository. This is similar to introducing the glossary recommended above.

The following is important because modelers allow the creation of model elements from graphical editors (thus making a diagram by filling the repository and visualizing the local instance), but also from the repository independently of any diagram. There, one must be vigilant when destroying an element, because if it is only destroyed locally in a diagram (in fact only the instance will be) the element will always be present in the repository.

In particular, beginners may find the relationships between elements tricky; in fact, the modelers respecting the SysML standard as best as possible forbid the construction of an incoherent model, which will be the case if a relation creates a conflict that is not visible but still present!

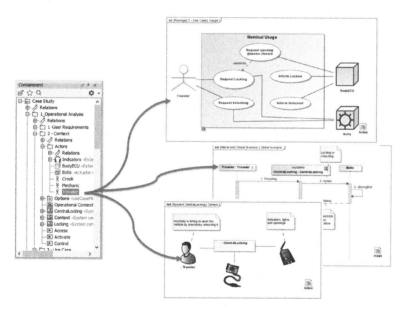

Figure 2.9. *Instantiation of a repository element in several diagrams. For a color version of this figure, see www.iste.co.uk/casse/sysml.zip*

2.7.1. *Difference between delete (Ctrl+D) and remove from diagram*

This difference is fundamental!

When you press the Delete key on your keyboard (often the Del. key on a QWERTY keyboard) in a diagram by pointing a symbol, you are only deleting this symbol, which is an instance of the Model represented locally.

The original element is always present in the repository.

If you want to erase the element completely, you must either type Ctrl+D as a shortcut, use the Edit menu command, or the icons on the palette.

Figure 2.10. *Locally or completely removing an element*

2.8. Stereotyping Blocks

The customization of symbols, especially their properties, is a series of relatively complex steps that we will discuss in a simple example.

CSM proposes a number of stereotypes applied to certain elements in order to ensure consistency with the MagicGrid approach, for example the Blocks can be more precisely identified as having a System, Domain, External, Context etc.

We will see later that a choice of colors can also be used to illustrate the use of a Block, such as Function or Component for example, belonging to the logical level and the physical level respectively.

We will add to the requirement element a "criticality" property that can have one of three values: "High, Medium or Low".

An exception, confirming the rule that you do not read a tutorial, is that this book is not intended to specify the use of the tool CSM in general, we will do it to illustrate the creation of stereotypes!

2.8.1. *Stereotype creation*

CSM imposes the creation of stereotypes in a profile; we will create one.

Figure 2.11. *Creation of a profile to store stereotypes*

By right-clicking in expert mode, we will use the command "Create Element", by typing the first letters of Package, the tool will propose a list of choices helping to find the correct name of the element or diagram to be created.

Then create a "criticality_Add" stereotype in this profile.

2.8.2. *Using an enumeration*

Our property can take one of the three values "High, Medium or Low", we will type our property as an enumeration. This enumeration will have three literals, we will call it "criticality_Enum".

2.8.3. *Label creation*

In the specification window of stereotype "criticality_Add", there is a field "Tag Definitions" which we will inform by creating a label "criticality", i.e. "criticality _Enum" as follows:

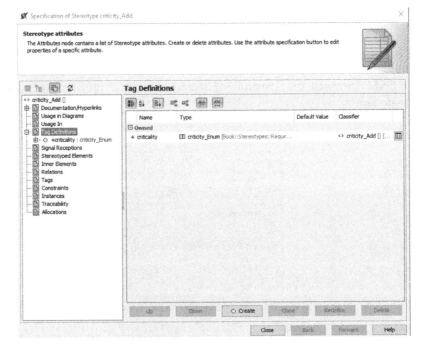

Figure 2.12. *Creation of a tag definition*

It is of course possible to create as many labels (Tag Definitions) as necessary. The possibilities of SysML extension and also customization of particular domains will be managed using stereotypes.

To help you identify the elements to create, Figure 2.13 is a representation of the model obtained.

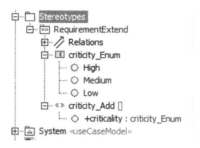

Figure 2.13. *Model obtained*

2.8.4. *Assigning value to the label*

We now have a stereotype applicable to any element (it is possible to restrict to a family of elements or to make this label available for all requirements; however, this is outside the scope of this book).

Figure 2.14. *Assigning a value to a label*

We will add our new label to an already existing requirement; just apply the stereotype we just created.

Then we will assign a value to our criticity label, by choosing one of the three possible values.

3

Example

Our case study is a centralized locking system for motor vehicles.

Figure 3.1. *A generic automobile vehicle*

Central locking is the access control system of a car. Locking is carried out on the doors, the boot and the fuel hatch.

This project is inspired by several types of centralization used by the author on his vehicles, of different brands. It is therefore not a particular version, the model being quite generic, even universal so that everyone can check on their own vehicle, similarities and differences.

3.1. User needs

Here we describe the different wishes and needs of the users targeted by our system. This set of expectations, gathered in a rather informal way, will be analyzed and transformed later into more formal and even contractual requirements, which in turn will serve as a basis for the system requirements that our model will have to satisfy.

What are the expected services of a central locking system fitted to a car? My first idea, as the user of the system, will be to secure access to this vehicle, allowing access only to the people to whom the owner of the vehicle has handed over the key, remote control, or whatever means chosen to execute this security. Securing will result in the locking of the opening preventing access to the inside of the vehicle (and the fuel hatch). For better convenience, the control of locking and therefore of unlocking, may be carried out by a mechanism linked to the start-up of the vehicle, another safety function preventing the starting of the engine, managed by another computer in the vehicle; we should not prematurely assume the final solution chosen, since a user does not have a very precise idea!

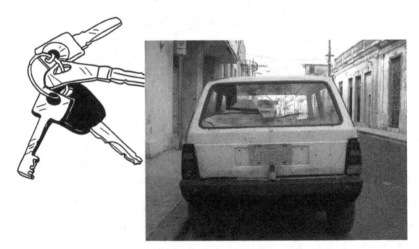

Figure 3.2. *A pragmatic locking system*

Thus, the ignition key seems to be an obvious (and very widely deployed) support, enabling the car to be locked or unlocked on a door or on the luggage compartment. This is likely to be the scenario of the

Example   85

initial use case. However, in a world with ever more wireless remote control systems, the possibility of a remote controlled system would be a very appreciable luxury. Also this remote control could bring additional services, i.e. operating equipment without sitting in the cockpit, or twisting to access different buttons. Other secondary scenarios may be envisaged, such as rainy days in the middle of the summer where one has to run to close the windows and sunroof which were left open to ventilate the car; here remote closing would be appreciated. Also, consider the situation when we visit friends in the countryside, without external lighting to guide us to reach the vehicle at night. Lighting the headlights remotely would also be appreciated.

3.2. Basic features

Control can be carried out in several ways:

– by remote control, often associated with the contact key, the most widespread mode, where remote controllers abandoned infrared transmission several years ago to a much more reliable radio link;

– passing one hand over the handle (non-contact system), ensuring that the unlocking of the vehicle will not happen accidentally if the badge holder is in the de-conviction or unlocking authorization zone;

– a control button on the dashboard, useful if the battery of the remote control or the badge is defective, to accommodate a passenger when the speed-based automatic shutter has activated, or as an emergency solution;

– automatic locking of the vehicle when its speed exceeds a certain threshold, to prevent any aggression by preventing access.

3.3. Variants (options)

Various options are mentioned, such as the closing of the glazed doors (on car doors, the roof), the lighting of the headlights during the journey from the car in a poorly lit place, the folding/deployment of the mirrors, automatic trunk opening, alarm management etc.

A major option is the contactless opening, with the replacement of the traditional contact key by a badge with a transponder. When this badge is detected at a "reasonable" distance from the vehicle, it can be opened by manipulating the access handles (no specific warning for the unlocking, this being done when opened in this case).

3.4. Constraints

The management of the system is generally spread over several computers (known as ECU – Electronic Control Unit), because it interacts with other vehicle functions. We will not go into detail about the interconnection of our system with the other ECUs, because often the architecture is specific to an automaker, where access to sensors and actuators depends on the availability of interfaces already specified for others systems, not to mention the mechanical stresses, overload, heat dissipation, cabling that should be taken into account. Our example will therefore use simplified interfaces.

The user (i.e. the driver) must have a feedback on the lock status of the automobile after command: locked or unlocked.

In a pragmatic way, in the pre-study phase resulting from the request received by the company that will be in charge of this system, we have analyzed a set of inputs and outputs that are necessary, *a priori*, for the functional aspects of our system, which are generally already present in most current vehicles. Nomenclature is intentionally generic, since more appropriate niche terms could have been used, and knowledge of networks embedded in a modern car would probably have guided us to choices of messaging using multiplexed networks instead of discrete inputs/outputs, or all-or-nothing that we have schematized here; we will refer to a model with essential borders. Supply does not appear.

We have also tried to be as independent as possible of the technologies used, for example on reception of the signal coming from the remote control or the badge, represented by a simplistic antenna.

Example   87

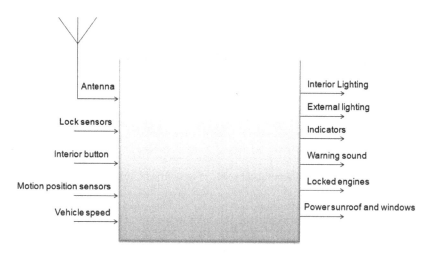

Figure 3.3. *The inputs/outputs of our locking system*

The main requirements of our system are listed in Table 3.1; they are derived from a spreadsheet, which also includes other attributes, including the unique identifier, which is useless at this level of presentation and not shown below.

Name	Description
Secure access	The user must be able to lawfully unlock and lock the car.
Securing objects	The user must be able to secure the doors and the fuel hatch.
Key Lock	The user must be able to control the system with a key.
Locking by Remote Control	The user must be able to control the system remotely.
Automatic locking	The user must be able to secure the vehicle automatically when taxiing.
Interior unlocking	The driver must be able to deactivate the system which has been locked automatically.
Safety release	In the event of an accident, the driver must be able to exit on his own or when he is rescued from the vehicle.
FollowMeHome lighting	The user must be able to obtain remote lighting assistance from the vehicle.

Rain protection	The user must be able to activate remotely the closing of the windows and the sunroof.
Locking Warning	The user must be able to be warned by one flash of the vehicle's unlocking hazard warning lights.
Unlocking Warning	The user must be able to be warned by two flashes of the vehicle's unlocking hazard warning lights.
Lock status	The user must be able to know the locking state, active or inactive.
Locking failure when stopped	The user must be able to be notified if locking is impossible.
Failure to lock when taxiing	If an opening prevents the automatic locking during taxiing, the user must be able to be warned by an alarm.
Open trunk transport	When an object is transported with the trunk open, the user must be able to force the internal locking.
Degraded mode	In the event of a system failure the user must be able to access the unlocked vehicle.

Table 3.1. *User requirements*

4

Case Study

4.1. Introduction

Before describing our case study, which we will develop in line with our generic approach, some additional aspects must also be taken into account. Since this chapter is definitely not a tutorial, the objective of each step will be explained, the analysis that allows us to obtain this result will be described and finally a screenshot of the diagram modeled in CSM will be presented.

4.1.1. *Key elements of modeling*

In SysML, the basic element manipulated is the block; we will devote a significant part of this book to this. Indeed, one of the main objectives of a model will be to describe the architecture of the system to be realized, while ensuring traceability with the expressed needs, the user requirements.

Another fundamental element is the relationship between elements, without of course underestimating the other symbols (activity, states, actors etc.).

Finally, naming and vocabulary guidelines must be established as early as possible. Strongly recommended in Requirements Engineering, the implementation of a glossary is also an indispensable reference in modeling. Cameo proposes the management of several glossaries (dictionaries) allowing the spell checking feature to avoid the use of misspelled (and therefore probably invalid) words in these glossaries.

4.1.2. Project structure

This section focuses on how to use the packages to store all the elements, which diagram and element(s) to use and when.

Based on the standard IEEE-15288 and some recommendations by INCOSE and MagicGrid, here is our suggested approach (also called methodology, process, etc.).

This approach is made up of four main categories, which in principle are sequenced (but iteratively), because the model will be structured according to the evolution of the project by successive iterations resulting from the analysis and synthesis of completeness, maturity and the relevance of the diagrams.

Each of these categories is broken down into steps for which we will provide an example based on our case study.

It is clear that efforts have been made to use the maximum number of elements and diagrams in the SysML toolkit, considered an integral part, and so an exhaustive overview was not sought.

Note that the illustrated approach is simplified; it does not intend to represent any particular methodology such as for an industrial project, but instead tries to respect the state of the art by taking a large number of steps observed during the consulting tasks carried out on several types of industrial client projects, from different fields.

The diagram in Figure 4.1 can be directly included in the CSM content diagram to guide the reader of the model by grouping and ordering the "useful" diagrams according to the context, the topic, and the contextual focus of the reader. Numerically prefixing the names of the diagrams can also reinforce this guidance.

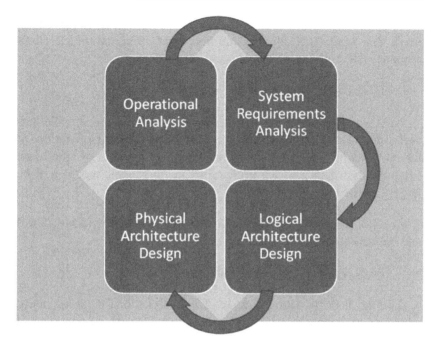

Figure 4.1. *Our generic approach*

The four main levels of our approach are therefore:

– Operational analysis:

Based on users' needs, objectives and activities, well before defining the system requirements, this level will be translated by the modeling of the objectives, the use cases and even the operational constraints.

We will study the internal block (ibd), sequence (sd), activity (act) and parametric (par) diagrams.

– System requirements analysis:

In this level, we will focus on modeling the outer limits of our system, its context, in principle represented in the form of a black box in order to identify interactions with other systems and users, one of the objectives being to estimate costs, feasibility etc.

We will study the tabular representation and the requirements (req), use case (uc), block definition (bdd), internal block (ibd), sequence (sd) and state machine (stm) diagrams.

– The design of the logical architecture:

Next we will consider one (or more) functional decompositions according to the technological choices envisaged, organization of internal/external realization (subcontracting), reuse of modules/ components/organs and the professions involved; this model will be largely linked to performance.

We will study the activity (act), sequence (sd), state machine (stm) and internal block (ibd) diagrams.

– The design of the physical architecture:

This level of modeling aims to define allocations to components, whatever their nature, which will be allocated to the disciplines of engineering.

We will study the internal block diagram (ibd) and the allocation table.

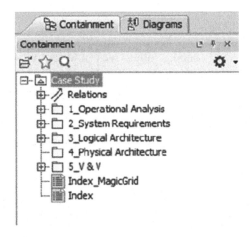

Figure 4.2. *Structuring the project using packages*

4.1.3. *Requirements characteristics*

It is customary to consider a requirement correctly expressed if its properties allow it to get the following characteristics:

Verifiable, clear and concise, complete, consistent, traceable, unambiguous, necessary, correct, feasible, atomic...

Here we are only speaking about requirements according to a precise framework and state of the art, transcribing what arises from the initial product idea or an expression of needs that is far too informal and therefore insufficiently contractual.

All of these requirements form a set of specifications for the project management teams. We listed our user requirements in Table 3.1; for our project this initial specification was created using a spreadsheet. Indeed, grouping the information in tabular (or matrix) form has many advantages, notably by relating the inter-element relations: allocations, traceability. The sorting of information will be greatly facilitated by a simple office tool that every engineer already uses.

In addition, many systems engineering tools can import or export data from or to spreadsheets to manage these spreadsheets.

4.1.4. *Stakeholder identification during the life cycle*

This step is not fundamentally linked to our MBSE approach, however it must be carried out at some point in the project (as soon as possible). Indeed it is with the stakeholders that we will gather the different needs and constraints in particular, with some stakeholders themselves being users of the future system. These users will appear as actors; CSM represents the actors with an image, so it is interesting to adopt a symbol as early as possible.

At the time of writing this book, version 1.5 of SysML had just become officially available. This version foresees the notion of "stakeholders" as a modeling element. This notion is useful for the points of view, discussed in section 1.20.

Figure 4.3. *Illustration of stakeholders. For a color version of this figure, see www.iste.co.uk/casse/sysml.zip*

Below are some examples of stakeholders in different life cycle stages:

– engineering: buyers, potential users panel, marketing division, R&D department, standardization body, suppliers, verification and validation team, production system, regulator/certification authorities, etc.;

– development: suppliers (component manufacture technical domains), design engineers, integration team, etc.;

– transfer for the control of production or quality of use, production system, operators, etc.;

– logistics and maintenance: supply chain, after-sales services, trainers, etc.;

– operation: normal users, unexpected users, etc.;

– disposal (withdrawal): operators, certification body, etc.

For our example, here are some potential stakeholders:

The customers, the automotive manufacturer (likely several divisions will be involved: marketing, architects, designers, security experts, etc.), the distribution and maintenance network, the insurance company, the usual or projected Tier 1 supplier, the standards concerned, etc.

Of course, all of these stakeholders will not use SysML directly, meaning that they are unlikely to create a model.

However, during the exchanges and proposals some diagrams can very advantageously specify the description (did Napoleon not say "A good sketch is better than a long speech"?).

It is therefore important to understand the meaning of certain diagrams and to share semantics.

4.2. Operational analysis

This step corresponds to the definition of the stakeholder needs, which is done conventionally by the drafting of requirements. The models can complement the text descriptions of the requirements, and we will see that SysML offers very interesting mechanisms for managing the links between these requirements and the modeling elements.

SysML coordinates the requirements with the rest of the model, storing their identifier and the descriptive text as basic properties. Like any SysML element, they can have a name. Finally, the most interesting aspect will be the possibility of assigning traceability links either to other requirements (by refinement of a different level, for example, or a hierarchical relationship) or also with other modeling elements, so as to justify any element created by a <<satisfy>> type link.

4.2.1. User requirements (table)

The use of requirements in a SysML model should not be a substitute for a requirement management tool dedicated or integrated into a global solution (ALM/PLM), a discipline of system engineering: requirements engineering. Indeed, it is essential to ensure the consistency of the model with these requirements via traceability on the one hand and on the other hand the textual description as the starting point of the analysis. We therefore only need to manage traceability links, and in order to do so have the identifiers of these requirements available, which is an essential reference for these requirements. We can therefore reserve a name, identifier, links and descriptive text (possibly even a navigation to the place, which preserves all the data relating to the requirements) in our model.

The validity of the creation of any modeling element will pass through the validation of a traceability link to these requirements, often indirectly by clarifying customer requirements by system requirements and also associated with a link to customer requirements. The creation of a non-traceable modeling element will have to be seriously justified!

4.2.1.1. Import of requirements

The main objective of this step is to ensure that traceability can be carried out as efficiently as possible.

There are several ways to import requirements stored in an external tool, through interfaces that allow the exchange by importing files or by communicating with the third-party tool API.

Here is a non-exhaustive list of possible interfaces with CSM: CSV (Comma Separated Values), Microsoft Excel, ReqIF, IBM DOORS Next Generation, PTC Integrity, Polarion, Siemens Teamcenter, or even Dassault Systèmes Catia.

A very practical feature is the ability to import by copy/paste, especially in cases of minor changes, without having to restart the entire import process.

One simply selects the information to be copied into the spreadsheet, here Microsoft Excel, and then pastes it into the CSM tabular window, as shown below.

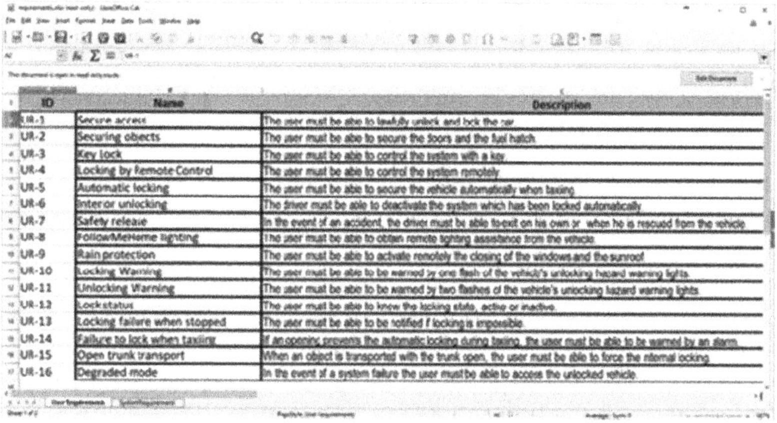

Figure 4.4. *Selecting requirement data in the source tool*

We will therefore create in our model a tabular view of the requirements, better suited for some information than a diagram.

In the CSM menu you will see in addition to the nine SysML diagrams, matrices and tables which are another form of representation.

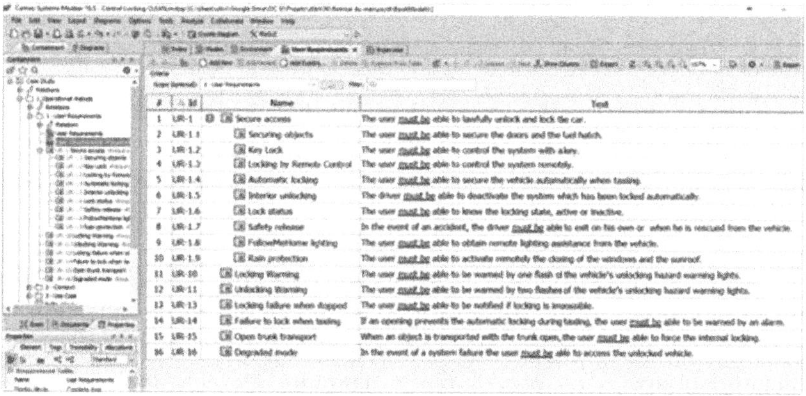

Figure 4.5. *Requirements imported into our model*

We will use a "requirement table" and after preparing the table so that its fields are compatible (order, name, type, etc.) we can paste the information, or even use the drag and drop, which is very convenient!

CSM has not only copied the information into the right place in the table, it has imported the requirements into our repository; they are now elements of our model, which can be linked to other elements in order to ensure their traceability.

For our case study we considered requirements with basic attributes, as provided by SysML, such as an identifier and the descriptive text of the requirement, in order to more easily identify our requirements; we have also added a name. For a real project, there would probably be a dozen (or more) attributes characterizing our repository. In this case, if we want to view or modify certain fields, it will be necessary to make the SysML requirement compatible with these attributes, by adding labels supported by a dedicated stereotype. Refer to section 2.8, which illustrates the creation of a stereotype and associated labels. This preparatory work of matching the requirements repository with the SysML profile of the project is the responsibility of a tool expert, under the control of the project manager deciding on the nature of this adaptation.

4.2.2. *Visualization of requirements (req)*

Even if we use this representation little (much preferring the tabular representation), it is possible to form boards illustrating the relationship between the requirements, either between them or with the other elements.

The choice of visualized elements must still be more relevant than for the other elements, because it is of course out of the question to represent all the requirements of a complex project (thousands!) and their relationships on one or more diagrams. Here, with our project being relatively simple (and simplified), it is possible to.

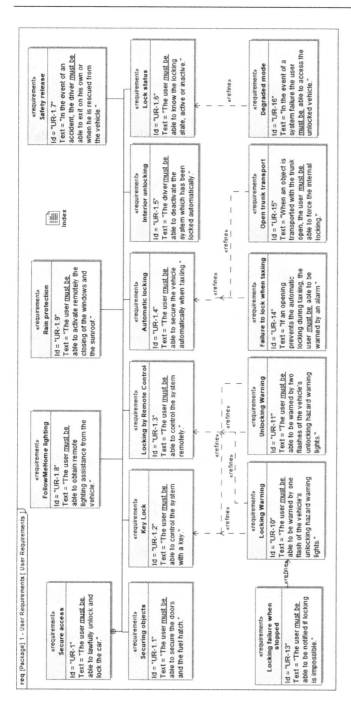

Figure 4.6. *Visualization of user requirements*

4.2.3. *Mission, vision and goals (uc)*

Modeling will make it possible to increase the readability, or even to better formalize certain requirements. These requirements come from a vision of the product to be achieved (its mission), that is, the definition of the target, the high-level goals. These goals will be the most abstract formulation of the requirements. The traceability of the requirements toward the goals will have to be ensured, however we will consider that it is the responsibility of the requirements engineering team, therefore not directly part of the MBSE approach. Refer to Chapter 3, describing our example topic.

Depending on the complexity and number of stakeholders involved in a project, it may be worthwhile to maximize its primary objective. This analysis is very interesting and will make it possible from the outset to initially agree on the overall system to be realized.

By reviewing the various documents available to us and gathering the opinions of the different stakeholders, we decided that the main actor of our system would be qualified as the "traveller", because the main objective of the system encompassing our subsystem, i.e. the vehicle, is to allow travel.

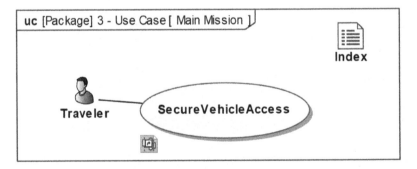

Figure 4.7. *Main project mission*

Then, looking more closely at the usages that the traveler expects from our system, it appears that he wishes to prohibit unauthorized access to the interior of the vehicle by blocking the accesses, but also to authorize chosen people to obtain this access. It is thus necessary to have a system enabling access to the vehicle to be granted only to persons in possession of an unlocking means, such as a key, badge, or by using a smartphone.

These same people (temporarily in the role of traveler) can also lock the vehicle again.

4.2.4. Context (bdd & idb)

The context diagram will allow us to imagine the system as a black box considering only the exterior. The context of the system consists of natural persons (typically users), existing systems (hardware, software), processes (business, technical or physical), events (physical or virtual) and documents (normative, regulatory).

It is important to dissociate the context of the system from its irrelevant environment.

The interfaces allow an exchange of information between the actors and the system.

These interfaces can be grouped under the term "actor", so we must identify the main actor as a priority and ultimately the secondary actors.

The initial analysis will be to identify the elements of the system environment, namely the external interacting elements essential to the system, in other words, the interacting persons, the business processes, as well as the legal, safety, security and "marketing" constraints in addition to the system's functional input-outputs. For this, we will go through the specifications to identify potential users and other systems in communication. In SysML these elements are grouped together as actors.

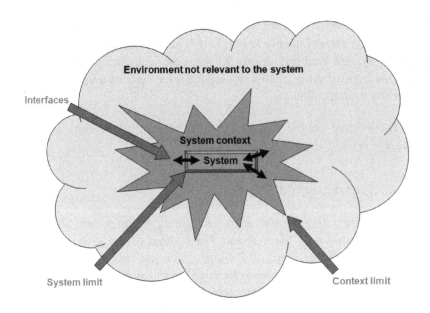

Figure 4.8. *System context. For a color version of this figure, see www.iste.co.uk/casse/sysml.zip*

Looking through the main document of our example topic, with the requirements in spreadsheet format, we find:

Driver, passenger, maintenance agent, direction change lights, windows and lighting. Also, for unwanted scenarios: an intruder or someone without permission to open the vehicle in order to steal it or steal objects.

Similarly, the construction of the system is likely to be entrusted to a tier 1 or even multi-functional equipment manufacturer if the functionalities are distributed among several physical systems. There are often statutory constraints (safety & regulation).

There are therefore two categories: human and system.

Let's take a closer look at human actors. A driver or a passenger seem to be good candidates for our main actor, yet an untrustworthy person, a maintenance technician and a rescuer are all likely to interact with our system.

Systems: should we specify the intermediaries, and describe them in detail, as for the various controls, remote controls and indicators? Ideally in a system engineering approach, we have to abstract the different elements where possible. In a modern automobile, it is clear that the many ECUs exchange a lot of data: our system is a perfect example. For the moment, we will take as a secondary actor "the rest of the vehicle" without going into further detail. We will refine this if necessary in the following steps, however much we classify this during consideration of the physical architecture as an assemblage of real computers, which are already known or conventionally used.

In passing, you will notice the use of the stylized stickman, most commonly observed for human actors and the substitution of this symbol by a "box" representation for the other non-human actors, most often subsystems. CSM makes it possible to replace this box with a much faster image to interpret, either from a library of stylized elements or from your own images.

We will refine our list of actors interactively by developing scenarios of exchanges between these actors and our system. For now, let us consider our main actor to be either driver or passenger (the traveler).

Then, as explained above, our system is integrated into a more global architecture, which is the complete motor vehicle, with a set of other subsystems, presumably ECUs, whose interfaces are already known. In our case, we know that the management of direction indicators (also known as blinkers) is managed by an ECU called the Body controller. It will therefore be necessary for our system to communicate with this computer, presumably by means of a specific vehicle protocol like the CAN or the LIN. As we know full well that these interfaces are imposed on us, that they are constraints that the stakeholders cannot question, do we from the start use real naming, physical characteristics and other attributes?

In modeling, one of the golden rules is to never try to obtain a comprehensive model, however, we may think that at some point in the project this stage of physical representation is necessary to minimize the (re)modeling effort. We may claim that creating the CAN bus messaging represents very important work for example, but will we completely need it?

It is therefore necessary to use the right level of abstraction, but it is not necessarily very simple!

In addition to our main actor "Traveler" and the Body ECU, we will manage the locks, which we could have considered as part of our system; it is a possibility that is discussed with the stakeholders.

This choice of architecture may not be realistic or optimal in a modern vehicle but our goal is to make our project compatible in other areas.

NOTE.– It is possible to apply stereotypes in SysML; it may be wise to collect the most useful in a profile, thus making them reusable. The same applies to value types (refer to section 2.8, illustrating the creation of a stereotype and its labels).

No Magic has provided predefined blocks in its SysML profile, which apply perfectly to an MBSE approach and CSM offers different block categories.

These can be adapted perfectly to our generic approach; we will use them for our model.

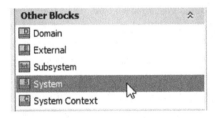

Figure 4.9. *Block categories proposed by CSM*

In SysML we will use a bdd to represent this black box, the interactions between the system and its direct environment, allowing the identification of actors (both human and material).

The use of a bdd involves the creation of a specific type of intermediate block, the <<system context>>, different from the block of the highest level, <<system>>, which could not be directly linked to the actors, not belonging to the system but to its context.

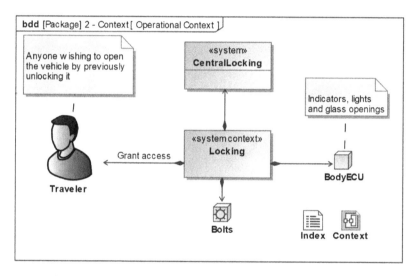

Figure 4.10. *Bdd operational context diagram*

A possible alternative, often used and preferred by the author, is to use an ibd that offers several advantages over the use of a bdd:

– the use of the <<system>> block as a pivot and black box, ensuring better consistency with the rest of the model (no creation of an "artificial" block to overcome a limitation of SysML);

– the possibility of specifying the actual interfaces and not the virtual relationships.

The creation of the internal block diagram will be done from the block of the highest level thus representing our system as a black box.

This block will also be used in other diagrams, notably the sequence diagram to identify the first exchanges between the main actor and our system.

Cameo Systems Modeler provides this type of block.

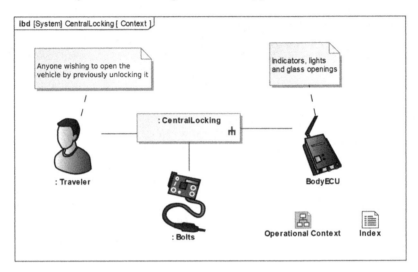

Figure 4.11. *ibd operational context diagram*

We have used images drawn in the integrated CSM library instead of the basic symbols, so these are not necessarily the most representative ones.

4.2.5. *Expected functionalities (uc)*

Here we will define the services that our system will provide for the main actor, with the aim of synthesizing the main "functions" to be ensured or how the system is used. These services are called Use Cases in SysML.

A good practice will be to use infinitive verbs to name each use case.

The two cases of use "Request Locking" and "Request Unlocking" correspond to the possibility for the traveler to solicit these requests.

As for the "Indicate Locking" and "Indicate Unlocking", they indirectly concern the traveler because it is the compartment controller that uses this service (to activate the turn signals in particular).

Also note the case "Request locking of glass openings" which also uses the passenger compartment as an extension to the main locking request, namely doors.

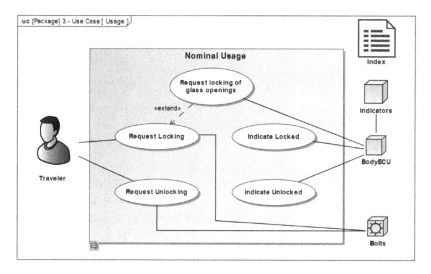

Figure 4.12. *Contextual use case diagram*

Note the use of different symbols for the system actors provided by CSM: "Actuator" and "External System".

We can also foresee the secondary use cases, corresponding for example to the options: alarm in case of intrusion, lighting for parking in the dark, etc. In this case, it is strongly recommended to use several diagrams in order not to mix too many cases, to modularize or even to share the project and above all to obtain legibility.

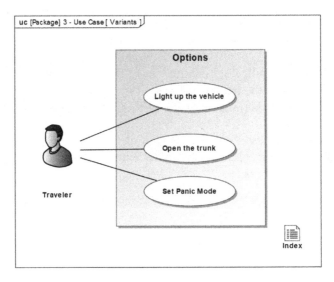

Figure 4.13. *Use case diagram of options*

4.2.6. *Use scenarios (sd)*

We can begin to assign nominal behavior to our "functions". These are scenarios that are steps sequence, in actions or objectives form. A textual representation is possible, even if the OMG does not impose or advocate any particular format for textual description of use cases, most SysML tools allow the entry of information as described by Alistair Cockburn in his book [COC 00], in particular, following a consensus of most users.

Here is an example of a possible framework:

Unique identifier, pre-conditions, post-conditions, assumptions, nominal and alternate or isolated processes.

It seems natural enough to describe these scenarios (nominal flow) using sequence diagrams:

– the traveler presses a button to unlock or lock the vehicle;

– the system generates a locking or unlocking action towards the locks;

– the locks return a status of success or failure of the operation;

– the traveler is informed of the status.

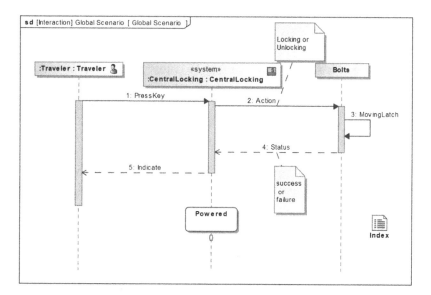

Figure 4.14. *Description of overall scenario*

This overall scenario is intentionally simplistic to anticipate a natural and very human defect, that of grasping too many details, and particularly attempting to grasp them too soon! Indeed, we are still in the black box version of our system, in the description of the problem and not yet in the description of the solution. Later, we will propose a more elaborate version when certain technological choices (or logical ones) are available.

4.2.7. *System modes (stm)*

During this stage, we will identify the main system modes, not to be confused with its behavior. For example initialization, calibration, diagnostics, standby, error, etc.

The term state will therefore be excluded because it is used in the state machines used to describe the behavior of a block; even if the two concepts are similar, their level of use being different, it seems important to differentiate them. Phase is used less. Some of the leading software systems in the embedded domain can be critical. These systems therefore include specific modes for managing failures. These are degraded modes, fallback strategies, resting strategies, etc. In the same way an initialization is often necessary, or even a calibration, a standardization, etc. What are these modes for our system? Let us analyze again the requirements to check if this is specified, in particular error cases and non-nominal functioning, i.e. the lack of battery voltage, a poorly closed door, etc.

This automaton of system modes is very similar from one project to another for the same domain; however, in some cases, it may be necessary to specify a number of very specific modes.

In the automotive field, for example, some ECUs are in standby mode in order to minimize the discharge of the battery. In critical areas, where human life can be in danger, the management of defects is paramount, for example fallback strategies must be implemented to ensure minimal functioning, to inform users and so on.

Conventionally, a system is supplied with electrical power, i.e. 115V/60Hz in the United States of America or in a motor vehicle 12V or 24V continuous for the most part.

We can therefore envisage two main modes: powered and non-powered. The unpowered state will be the default mode and simplified to the extreme, our system being normally inactive. The powered mode will be decomposed in such a way as to support an operational mode, one that each user will be able to anticipate, then fault management, error reports and in some cases a calibration and standardization phase (for measuring instruments), diagnostics, etc.

In a car, there are modes that can be identified by computers in order to control their activity and therefore their consumption: vehicle stopped and engine off, engine started, contact set and low battery. In the automotive field, several system variables are provided to indicate these modes: KL15, KL30 or KL50, as shown in the diagram below.

For our system itself, it might be interesting to identify problems or even breakdowns that could lead to a malfunction.

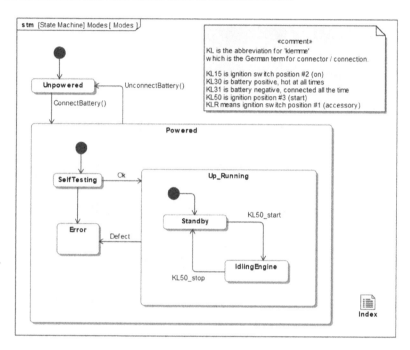

Figure 4.15. *System modes*

The most common case for a centralized locking system is the incorrect closing of a door preventing locking from taking place.

Is this a malfunction or simply an example of use that the system must be able to manage and can the traveler be warned that locking is impossible?

It is probably too early to specify whether the behavior of the system is different in the case of bad behavior of the traveler (door badly closed) or a sensor, a locking electromotor, wiring fault, etc.

On the other hand, using a current measurement, for example, it would be possible to verify, before any request, whether the system is fully operational.

4.3. System requirements analysis

In this step, we will go through the requirements from the various stakeholders, the previously imported User Requirements, in order to analyze those we will derive into System Requirements. We will still be in the black box version of our system, however we will begin our analysis of the functional architecture. The main objectives of this stage are to ensure a good understanding of the demand of the project manager, its feasibility and the quantification of the effort required.

This step is essential for the continuation of the project, as the transformation into technical requirements of the initial specification from the user's point of view will ensure its proper understanding. We thus obtain the following list:

Name	Description
Central locking	The system must allow a user to unlock and lock his car.
Locking targets	Locking acts on the doors and the fuel hatch.
Key lock	The system must be able to be controlled by a key.
Locking by remote control	The system must be able to be remotely controlled.
Radio power	The operating range of the remote control must be at least 10 m (33 ft) and at most 25 m (82 ft).
Automatic lock	The system must automatically lock the vehicle when the speed of 20 km/h (12.5 mph) is reached.
Inner unlocking	When the system is locked automatically, the system allows the driver to deactivate it.
Automatic unlocking	When the system is locked automatically, the system must disable it in the event of an impact that reveals a road accident.
Semi-automatic unlocking	When the system is locked automatically, the system must disable it if one of the doors is opened from the inside.

Interior lighting	After the vehicle is unlocked, the system must turn on the vehicle interior lighting for 3000 ms.
Remote lighting	The system must allow a user to light the dipped beam and interior lighting for 30000 ms remotely.
Closure of openings	The system must allow a user to close the windows and roof by the locking function.
Warning by flashing lights	The system must inform the user by the hazard warning lights of the vehicle's locking or unlocking.
Unlocking warning	One flash for unlocking.
Locking warning	Two flashes for locking.
Door status Indicator	When the ignition is turned on, a warning light indicates that the doors are locked and, if not illuminated, that they are unlocked.
Hands-free mode	In addition to the lights, an audible signal.
Poor closure	If a door or trunk is not properly closed, the system must warn the user that locking is impossible.
Closure fault	No audible signal or flashing hazard warning lights.
Override of the open compartment	When the object is to be transported with the open compartment, the system must allow a long press on the internal locking to lock.
Faulty system	In case of failure the system must leave the vehicle unlocked.

Table 4.1. *System requirements*

We will now create a derivation table of the User Requirements for our new System Requirements. In Cameo Systems Modeler, this table is called Derive Requirement Matrix. It is fundamental to be able to move between these two levels because when a requirement needs modifying, this will be the only way to carry out an impact analysis.

Figure 4.6 simply presents the User Requirements (columns) and System Requirements (rows).

It is interesting to note that several User Requirements are covered by more than one System Requirement, for example "Remote Locking" is covered by six System Requirements.

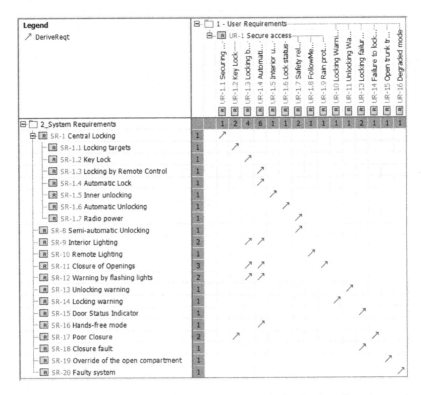

Figure 4.16. *Derivation table of User Requirements for System Requirements*

4.3.1. *External interfaces (ibd)*

This section will allow us to outline our system by determining what its interfaces are and what elements interact with it, considering it in the form of a black box.

We have already identified the actors using the context diagram, without specifying what is exchanged between these actors and our system. We must now look at the fluids, energies, materials or data that our system receives or produces. We can already anticipate that what is exchanged will be radio waves and electric waves with no pneumatic or hydraulic phenomena to be managed.

At the input, remote control signals can be of high frequencies (infrared management is almost unused today); for badges, transponders will use a similar technology; and communication with other computers will require data (transported electrically on Bus LIN or CAN).

At the output, we will also have communication with other computers and, power management for electric motors.

Depending on the manufacturer, it is likely that the overall architecture of the vehicle is already established and that our interfaces are frozen and may even be imposed.

Our company (I identify both the reader and myself as part of this company) may have already produced the computer with which our system will communicate: in this case, we master the interfaces perfectly. However, it seems more likely that there is a multi-vendor supply and that good interoperability is to be ensured independently of the vendor, which means that the interfaces will be formally specified by a set of requirements that we will use.

We anticipated that several variants (options) were possible; depending on their characteristics, the interfaces may evolve, so, to ensure the best operability, it is therefore essential to predict all the cases, even if we oversize (not too much, as this is expensive) connectivity for future developments.

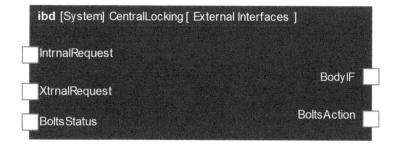

Figure 4.17. *External interfaces of the system*

Here, we will use an ibd in an ultra-simple black box, typing the input-output ports directly on the ibd.

Note the change of colors: black background symbolizing the black box, white text for the best contrast.

4.3.2. System scenarios (seq - act)

Now that we have detailed the input-output, we will more accurately describe the interactions between our system and the outside world; we will only focus on the solution, with constrained choices, for the ports whose typing is known. From the sequence diagram (possibly several), we will obtain our inital activities or functions.

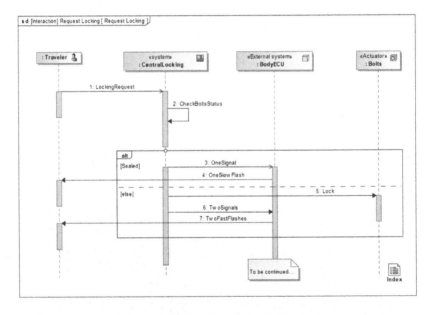

Figure 4.18. *Locking request diagram*

Here we have chronologically detailed the first or second use case, when a new user appears in the vicinity of a vehicle.

We focus on the system exchanging with its environment from the point of view of the traveler.

We obtain potential candidates in terms of functions, represented here by SysML operations. These operations are created on the "system" block.

In order to ensure traceability between all these steps, we will progressively document and justify the links between these activities, resulting from our analysis, with the user requirements imported at the start of the project. This is an excellent technique to also obtain an impact analysis when changing user requirements.

Here is a list of candidate operations:

– SendOneSignal and SendTwoSignals may use the same communication function with BodyECU; this will be fine-tuned.

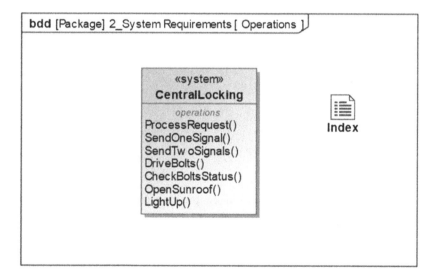

Figure 4.19. *Main operations*

4.3.3. *Functional traceability (table)*

CSM proposes a table called Satisfy Requirement Matrix which we consider appropriate to manage traceability as early as possible. We will therefore ensure that the candidate operations meet the user requirements previously imported by this means. We create a SysML Satisfaction Matrix by selecting the operations as rows and the requirements as columns. We then obtain the following table. By double clicking on intersections, CSM will automatically create a <<satisfy>> link. We can move on to the next step when all our operations cover at least one requirement. Otherwise, we need to review our analysis.

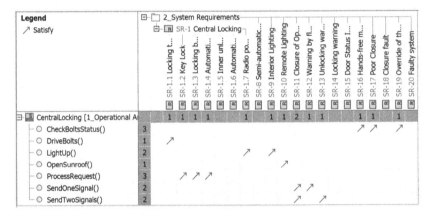

Figure 4.20. *Functional traceability*

The exercise seems to have been properly carried out, since our operations are assigned to at least one requirement, but some requirements are not covered; it would be good to ensure that we do not forget to take all of them into account. In fact, it would appear that the hierarchy of requirements has not been sufficiently validated; it would be necessary to use the containment relation to manage the overlaps, thus forming a tree, which would make it possible to verify if the lower level, only relevant in this case, is covered.

4.4. Logical architecture design

The objective of this step is to design a functional architecture model satisfying the requirements and describing the system to be realized; here we are clearly entering the field of the solution, the system becoming a white box.

It is therefore a matter of dealing with "what" without specifying "how" (too much) and doing so in a logical way.

What function? There does not seem to be any direct equivalent in SysML!

INCOSE defines a function as a task, action, or characteristic activity that must be accomplished to achieve a desired result. Action and activity are indeed SysML keywords that we know, so the functional side of a system is located in this area.

4.4.1. *Main functions (act)*

Here we assign an activity to each operation of the "system" block.

The system block includes operations which are used in the initial sequence diagram; here the behavior is refined by an activity diagram.

Since the previous level, we have already identified several candidates for our activities:

– ProcessRequest, SendOneSignal, SendTwoSignals, DriveBolts, CheckBoltsStatus, OpenSunroof and LightUp.

With regard to the last two, it seems appropriate to group them under one name: Issue Warning.

Finally we opt for the creation of six activities, used in the following figure in an activity diagram.

It will be necessary to describe the behavior of each: activity diagram, state machine diagram, sequence diagram etc.

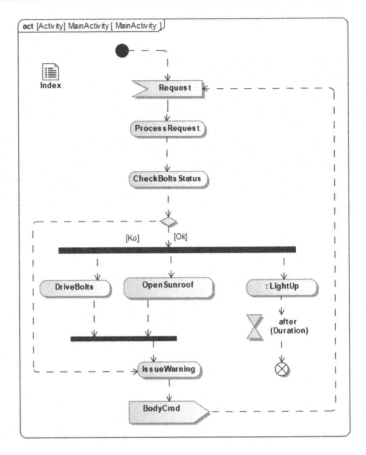

Figure 4.21. *Main activity diagram*

4.4.2. *Internal interfaces (ibd)*

It is appropriate in this step to create blocks in an ibd, by retrieving the higher input-outputs, in the system frame, each block being responsible for processing one or more inputs in order to generate one or more outputs.

NOTE.– In reality, we do not create a block directly in an ibd, because in this diagram we only manage parts and references. However, CSM will automatically create these blocks for you, as soon as you create these parts or references without any existing typing, i.e. without a previously created block, either in the repository or in a bdd.

The request in this step, as already mentioned above, is to choose between an abstract and theoretical representation of the input and output signals. For example, the request (locking request, unlock request, lighting, etc.) must come from the main actor or be considered as a message from the remote control subsystem or badge handled by the traveler.

It would seem wise to use the first form for the problem domain and the second for the solution domain, or the first case as the black box level and the second case as the white box. Be careful not to use different levels of abstraction.

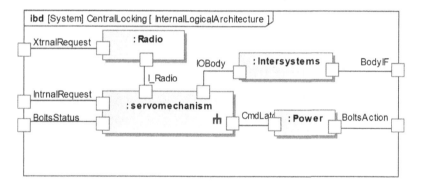

Figure 4.22. *ibd logical architecture, start of white box*

NOTE.– The parts shown in Figure 4.22. are not named. Indeed, the reference prefixed by a colon points to its type, in this case the type of a part is a block. It is therefore an instantiation; it may be wise in certain situations to name these instances, especially when there are many in order to differentiate them.

4.4.3. *Typing ports*

With regard to the choice of the abstraction level, as mentioned on the previous page, the choice of the typing must be consistent and, in the behavioral description part of each block, this choice will be extremely decisive and involve major modifications to our modeling. Advance carefully.

One of the first choices made upstream was the typing of inputs/outputs, if we have opted for "real" typing, we must be coherent, and so it would be wrong to opt for a more abstract level in a downstream stage. On the other hand, we must ensure a good coherence with the "internal" ports, which we understand to be those we create by altering the architecture of the white box.

The direction that is displayed on the port is actually the combination of the direction of the properties of the flows belonging to the block typifying the port, so we have defined "proxy" ports by associating them with interface blocks, to position the directions as we wish. Here a bdd is used, mainly due to convenience, but also for its documentary role.

Logically, the requests are incoming, similarly for the locking state, and the action on the locks is outgoing; on the other hand, the interface with the Body ECU of the passenger compartment is bidirectional, because messages are exchanged in both directions.

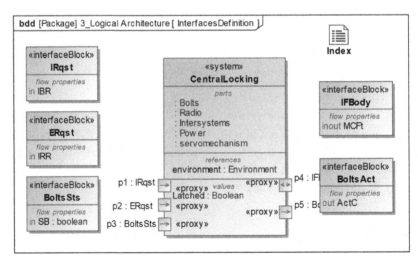

Figure 4.23. *Choice of port directions*

NOTE.– Prior to SysML 1.3, the flow ports, obsolete in SysML 1.3, allowed a direction to be "manually" chosen.

In the ibd diagram in Figure 4.20, illustrating our early logical architecture, the port categories as well as their direction have been automatically updated.

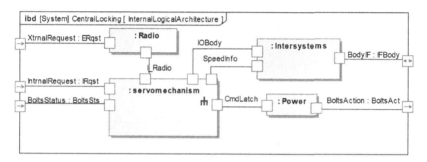

Figure 4.24. *ibd logical architecture update after refinement of external ports*

NOTE.– That the control part servomechanism is decomposed (fork symbol). In fact we have discovered that several state machines would be necessary for its behavioral description, so we prefer to assign them to blocks (and therefore to the parts), so we do not use the notion of parallelism.

4.4.4. Flows

Perhaps an answer to the question of how to type the ports, flows can indeed specify what is conveyed by their flow elements. We will probably have two types of signals: messages and power control, still to be specified.

4.4.5. Block behavior

In our SysML toolbox we have several ways of describing a behavior, which we have already mentioned, so we will try to choose what we feel is most appropriate.

4.4.5.1. *Radio*

This block is responsible for transforming the signals received by the radio module or by the transponder in the case of a contactless access badge.

The type of behavioral diagram that seems most suitable to describe the dynamics of block is the activity diagram. Indeed, it is a sequence that transforms a high-frequency radio signal into locking and unlocking commands (or even some additional orders, for example, closing the sunroof) according to the system variant.

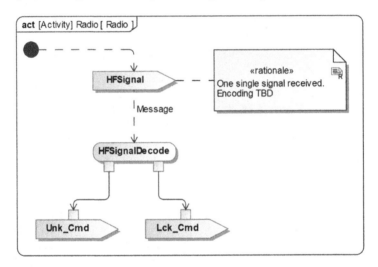

Figure 4.25. *Block radio signal*

4.4.5.2. *Control*

This block is broken down into three sub-blocks to specify a behavior for each of the blocks corresponding to the final vehicle configuration. Indeed, as explained above, we want to avoid the use of orthogonal states, preferring to "specialize" a state machine (or other behavior) using blocks. We benefit from both modularity and traceability.

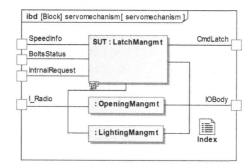

Figure 4.26. *Decomposition of the control block*

The Lock Management Block receives the external (transformed by the radio block) and internal requests (button on the dashboard) for unlocking and locking the vehicle.

It also receives additional requests for deadlocking (involving the closing of the sunroof), lighting and possibly panic mode triggering the vehicle's alarm.

It transmits lock management commands and direction indicators.

This is the core of our system that will contain control logic. A state machine thus seems an excellent way to describe this.

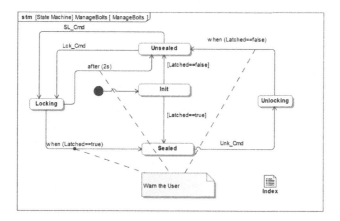

Figure 4.27. *State machine for locking management*

NOTE.– To construct the diagram, it is advisable to drag/drop the elements as much as possible from the confinement tab, for example, for the triggers "Lck_Cmd" and "Unk_Cmd". In case of renaming, the changes will be propagated in the diagrams where these elements are referenced because, by entering their names in the diagram, the link would be broken.

The sunroof and windows management block will be very simple.

Finally, the external lighting control unit will have the objective of remotely controlling the headlights for a duration corresponding to the number of presses on the control in full light (but is this in the specification?).

4.4.5.3. Power

This block is a kind of relay without real "intelligence", transforming the locking and unlocking commands into a signal powerful enough to actuate the locking motors. A parametric diagram is very simple to represent this functionality. We will use the universal torque equation $T = K_1I^2 + K_2V^2 + K_3\ VI^{\cos(phi\text{-}tau)} + K$. T represents the torque, K a coefficient, I the current, V the voltage.

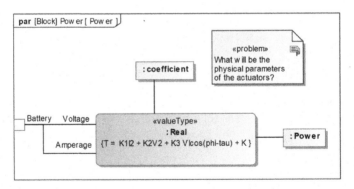

Figure 4.28. *Parametric power diagram of locking motors*

4.4.5.4. Inter-systems

This block is used to adapt the signals coming from our system to those expected by its environment, i.e. other computers. At this stage, we do not have sufficient information on the architecture of the vehicle to detail this block.

4.4.6. Tabular allocation and traceability (table)

As we saw in section 2.3.3, we will ensure the traceability of the elements created in this step with those from the previous steps. Here we must ensure that the architecture elements analyzed can satisfy the System Requirements.

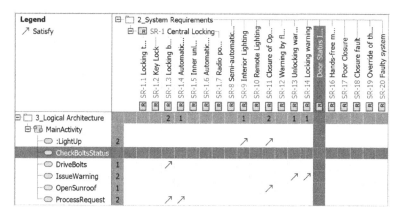

Figure 4.29. *Traceability matrix for satisfaction of requirements by activity*

4.5. Physical architecture design

In this step we will model the physical architecture model with the different components, organs, equipment, computers, etc. which make up the system with the links between these different components. We will also describe the functions by one or more components for this level of realization.

SysML is not adapted for the management of the installation characteristics of components, in particular the bulk, weight, volume, radiation, heating, etc. for which CAD tools (Computer Aided Design) will be more suitable. That said, the tooling can help the study of different possible options during allocation, according to certain constraints expressed by the requirements. This roll-up analysis is necessary for creating nomenclature and, in the field involved, weight, cost and consumption are critical characteristics of a product. By quantifying and weighting these properties, this calculation will be a valuable asset for the project team. This type of calculation is often done by a spreadsheet or by "house" tools.

CSM offers this kind of functionality by equipping the calculation (the most common sum) of the properties (values) of the blocks.

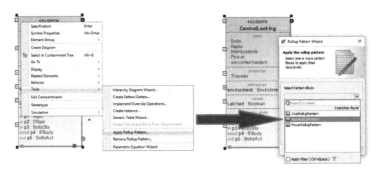

Figure 4.30. *Roll-up analysis (cost, mass, consumption)*

At this stage of the project, the artifacts in our model may be used mainly to produce a specification document. The consistency of the model, the possibility of verifying/validating certain aspects, are less questionable. However, with ever more projects targeting leading software systems, it is tempting to want to reuse certain diagrams (notably state machines) in order to generate the code corresponding to the algorithms specified and thus verified/validated (provided that the model was originally provided for this purpose). Some modeling tools (SysML or not) natively propose the ability to generate code, which will be arranged in series, i.e. a generated production code. The code generation techniques have been developed for several decades; the tools are also high performing and the code meets the quality and maintainability criteria without problems. A major challenge in most cases is the extra cost of the required code size compared to manual writing. However, this depends on the criticality of the applications, the complexity of the project, etc.

Returning to the generation of state machine code, another important challenge is the conformity of the action language used with the type of target code, for example, the code C is very widespread in automotive ECUs. In C, the notion of signal or event does not exist; as with any computer language, the data are based on information of constant or variable nature: integers, real, booleans, tables, etc.

We have seen that the semantics of state machines in SysML is based on the synchronization upon receipt of a "pure" signal, representing the moment a button is pressed, for example, or even a "system" signal, including the expiration of a timer.

How then can the compatibility of the signal be maintained with the information received from the sensors and sent to the actuators?

There are several techniques, such as adding two buffer stages to system inputs and outputs to convert physical signals into SysML-compliant information. This can prove tedious in the case where a large number of signals are present, however relatively simple to implement.

The basic recipe is simple: imagine an electrical signal (not our SysML signal) coming from an all-or-nothing sensor, in a car, of either 0V or 12V.

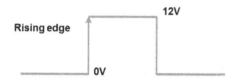

Figure 4.31. *Symbolization of an electrical signal*

We have to transform this signal, which we can call analogue, into "logic" information that our SysML model can interpret, signal or event. To do this, we have a keyword in the toolbox: "when ()". In our example, the presence or absence of battery voltage of the vehicle, i.e. 12V, the event to be generated will therefore be synchronized on the change from 0V to 12V with "when (voltage_sensor==12)" and vice versa (voltage_sensor==0).

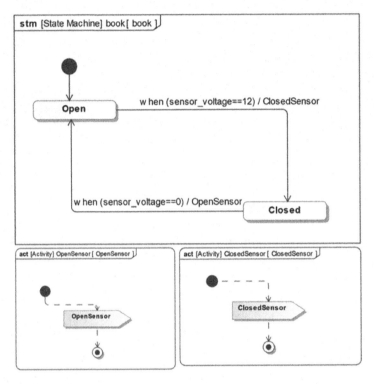

Figure 4.32. *Transformation of an electrical voltage value into a SysML signal*

Each effect is associated with an ultra simple activity chart, since it emits only the signal of the same name.

4.5.1. *Candidate solutions*

The balanced distribution of the different components is a trade (that of architect), which we will not discuss in this book. There are a large number of possible solutions: if the functions to be implemented will be largely software-based, and the interfaces are "standard", i.e. already provided on an existing computer, this will probably be a cheaper solution. On the contrary, if it is a question of innovative or competitive functions, the production of this in-house equipment would certainly make sense, or it could be that subcontracting would be more suitable.

For our solution, we will choose to use a "controler" computer equipped with two daughter cards, one for managing the radio part in connection with the remote control or the hand-free badge, the other for the wired interfaces, power for locking and network for intercommunication in the vehicle.

This gives us the following very simple architecture where we have deliberately not specified ports which we will discuss below.

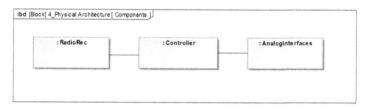

Figure 4.33. *The three physical components in the system*

4.5.2. *Physical interfaces (ibd)*

In our automotive example, the integration of system notes (a subsystem at the vehicle level) will be based on the availability (and preliminary definition) of the existing interfaces: all or none or nothing, bus CAN, LIN, OBD2 for diagnostics, FlexRay, MOST, etc.

It seems unlikely that the choice of technologies will be made during this stage, as they are most likely to be specified as early as possible, as described in section 2.3; the logical representation of these interfaces may not have been carried out but, identifying the physical interfaces with the other subsystems or even the manufacturer's recommendations in this area should be carried out at the start if possible.

4.5.3. Constraints (par)

Here the idea will be to ensure a link to multi-physical tools, allowing the link between our "reactive and discrete" SysML model with other "continuous" models used to supplement standard control law algorithms.

4.5.4. Tabular allocation and traceability (table)

Once again, we will use a table to document the transpositions carried out in the form of an allocation matrix:

– The Physical Blocks (X-axis) and the Functional Blocks (Y-axis).

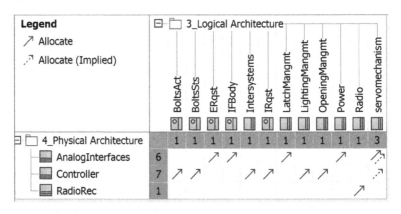

Figure 4.34. *Component Allocation Table with Function Blocks*

Beyond Modeling

5.1. Verification and validation of models

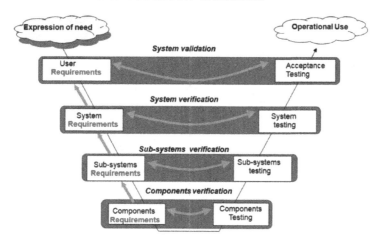

Figure 5.1. *V cycle: validation and verification. For a color version of this figure, see www.iste.co.uk/casse/sysml.zip*

5.1.1. *Validation or verification?*

Among all the techniques used to test a model, it is important to distinguish between validation and verification as well as the system test itself, which may be one of the objectives of the model (or one of its variants). Let us list the different possibilities.

NOTE.– Here, we will distinguish between the validation and verification of the model from those of the system; we will see how the two domains are interconnected of course since they are very strongly linked:

– *static*: this technique often consists in ensuring that the consistency and the completeness of the model are correct, by controlling rules established in this sense. Control is based on element types, relationships, properties and so on, without requiring execution or simulation;

– *dynamics*: the technique allows the testing of various hypotheses during the execution of the model, by stimulating the inputs and inspecting the outputs;

– *prototyping*: here the model is used in a simulation or physical apparatus in order to reconstitute near-real-life conditions;

– *review*: this technique uses the eyes of experts to analyze the content of the model;

– *formal methods*: techniques that are rather difficult to implement with a SysML model, they allow mathematically to demonstrate the conformity of the model;

– *traceability*: required to complete a static verification with elements external to the SysML model, primarily requirements but above all the expression of needs.

5.1.1.1. Verification

Most SysML tools have a static model consistency verification module. CSM provides one that allows each step of creating modeling elements to ensure conformity to the standard and homogeneity of the model.

It is recommended to perform this type of check regularly, especially before performing a validation by execution of the model.

In the diagram editor tool palette (Figure 5.2), next to the zoom buttons, there is a "Validate Diagram" button to apply a set of check rules on the current diagram.

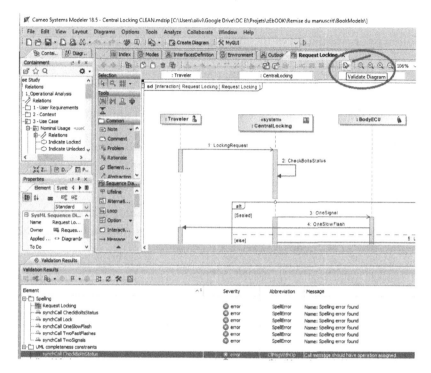

Figure 5.2. *Validating the diagram. For a color version
of this figure, see www.iste.co.uk/casse/sysml.zip*

Here, if errors have been found, a results window containing the
nature of the error and a description is displayed. Right-clicking on the
element to be corrected will contextually allow you to navigate to this
element, correct the error (in some cases automatically) depending on
the context, or even ignore it, even if this is to be avoided!

NOTE.– The test carried out locally from the diagram editor is more
exhaustive than the global test carried out by the Menu Analyze
-> Validation -> Validate. Indeed this test has fewer rules to not
penalize performance, but it is possible to parameterize it.

It is recommended to run this test after the local test to check the
impact on the entire model.

NOTE.– Why validation and not verification at this level? The following is validation of the model.

5.1.1.2. *Validation*

The objective here is to ensure that the model satisfies a given problem, that is, it conforms to a set of specific requirements.

As such, the execution of the model can be considered a validation, as this ensures that the model implements the expected behavior of the system or the absence of defects in the description.

CSM allows the use of certain numerical values contained in the requirements to control the simulation. These values can be compared to the values obtained.

CSM relies on a glossary of terms equivalent to mathematical comparison operators such as: equality, less than, greater than, etc. For example, the most useful terms are "equal to", "greater than" and "less than". The terms in the glossary are highlighted in the requirements document (see Figure 5.4)

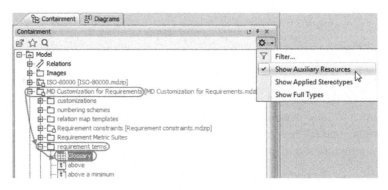

Figure 5.3. *Access to the glossary in SysML. For a color version of this figure, see www.iste.co.uk/casse/sysml.zip*

If a Block contains a value constrained by a requirement, a satisfaction link from the block to the requirement will allow the simulator to validate compliance with this requirement dynamically.

Figure 5.4. *Use of a term present in the glossary*

Then during the simulation, the color of the obtained value will be green, if the requirement is satisfied, and red in the opposite case. Similarly, constraints containing a quantifiable value will see their color evolves according to whether they meet the requirement or not. It is a function essential to the validation of requirements and constraints (which are a kind of non-negotiable requirement, refined or imposed) when estimating system parameters, changes in values supported by the Blocks, etc.

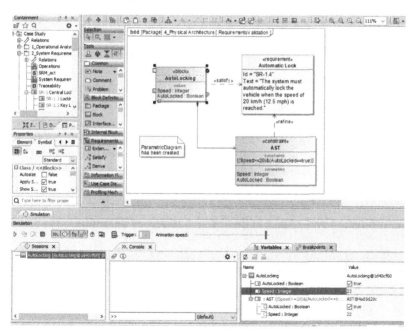

Figure 5.5. *Coloration of values associated with constraints.*
For a color version of this figure, see www.iste.co.uk/casse/sysml.zip

5.1.2. *Execution of the model*

The technology used involves an interpretation engine, and other methods, including the generation of compilable and executable code; however, interpretation has many advantages in MBSE.

In the first place, the completeness of the model is not an obstacle, and the wrong use of the action language syntax will not block the simulation either. There is also no need to ensure the presence of the right compiler, with the right version to generate an executable model. A simulation by code generation will nevertheless have a clear advantage over the speed of execution; however, with current computer power, this does not represent a decisive advantage in balancing the advantages.

CSM proposes to run several diagrams; for some it does not make sense, especially structural (or static) diagrams, although these levels are used to define the execution field, because the Blocks contain the definitions of the values, including the variables that will be updated during execution, which also include, for example, the behavior of state machines and define the number of instances that will be created, reflecting the multiplicity of parts contained by the Block. However, as far as animation is concerned, we will see that CSM proposes a rather nice functionality that is to be able to visualize and follow exchanges on the streams by ports, for example.

For the behavioral part, which is certainly the most interesting, CSM proposes to simulate the state machine diagram, activity diagram and the activities described by an action language that is executable (script or computer) in the operations, activities, etc. Similarly the execution of the simulation can appear in the form of sequence diagrams.

With its simulation module, CSM allows tools to control execution, choose the context, view/modify values, generate events and functions known in a standard debugging tool. In order to improve the ergonomics and not to manipulate only elements of the model too abstractly, it is possible to connect to the simulation interfacing panels in which buttons will generate events, view/edit values a lot more simply and quickly.

NOTE.– The timing of execution of a model, including a state machine, will be at the trigger fire, in other words, if there is no event in the transition but only a guard, when the value returned by a Boolean expression [guard] becomes true, the transition will not be executed. The keyword when() or the association of an event, for example after(duration),will also make the transition executable.

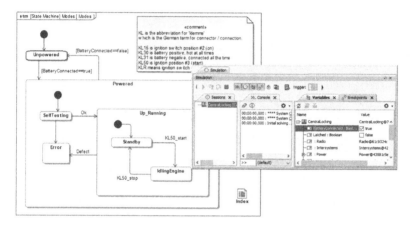

Figure 5.6. *Change in value of a guard*

In the diagram above, the change of value of the Boolean Battery Connected is not taken into account, in the absence of a trigger fire. Several modeling techniques are possible to avoid this problem, the transformation by the keyword when (Battery Connected) is undoubtedly the most elegant, which transforms the change of value into signal. If another state machine contained in the simulation profile contains a reflexive transition (causing the source state to be looped back) with thekeyword after(),thus enabling the update of transitions, the overall use of guards will be possible.

A simulation profile can be created, we will describe one simulating the state machine of the block "LockManagement".

5.1.2.1. *Execution without profile*

A right click on "ControlLocking" in our diagram will allow us to launch a local simulation. A fairly simple and intuitive simulation control panel then appears; the button in the shape of green arrow to run, the red square to stop (Figure 5.7).

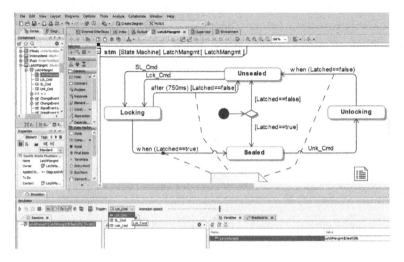

Figure 5.7. *Execution of a diagram. For a color version of this figure, see www.iste.co.uk/casse/sysml.zip*

Note that CSM proposes in a drop-down list, the list of trigger elements available in context.

Let us execute by clicking on the green arrow to the far left, the initial pseudo-state is traversed, the tool stops on the decision symbol by highlighting it in red, indicating the active state (or pseudo-state here).

Thanks to the interpreted mode, the simulation mode is relatively lenient and does not stop in case of indeterminism or evaluation of untyped elements; on the contrary CSM even proposes to choose which branch to follow.

Indeterminism will occur if you have not taken care to exclusively set the default value "Latched" or if you have not (yet) typed this value by a Boolean.

In our case, the interactive simulation is purely local, which means that the typing of the variables, i.e. the values belonging to the Block supporting the state machine are also unknown, the Boolean "Latched" is therefore perceived as text, not only without a type but also without value. The simulator then detects an indeterminism.

NOTE.– It is strongly recommended that you start the simulation from the Block that includes the state machine and then open the state machine to animate it. A more complete scope will allow the simulator to evaluate the values correctly. Of course, the use of a profile, described below, for a larger model, will not have these drawbacks.

Choosing "Latched==false", by answering "Yes" to the question asked, we logically switch to "Unsealed" status. Then by choosing from the trigger drop-down list the "Lck_Cmd" element we will find ourselves in the Locking state and so on.

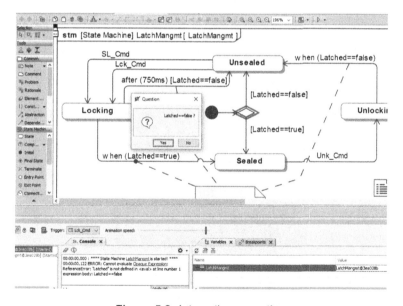

Figure 5.8. *Interactive execution*

By right clicking on an element, here a transition or a state, it is possible to set a breakpoint (Simulation menu). Another right click on the variables tab will allow you to create a runtime sequence diagram.

5.1.2.2. *Execution with profile*

With this profile we can integrate all or part of the model and, in particular, associate a graphic panel (HMI) to stimulate our model and visualize the results.

The approach is similar to that used in a tool such as Visual Basic, for example. CSM has a specific type of diagram (a profiling in fact dedicated to the simulation): the Simulation Configuration Diagram.

We create it in a dedicated package, always for the rigorous accessibility to the elements of our model. We also need a User Interface Modeling Diagram in which CSM has created a simulation configuration. The target must be accurately defined, in our case the block containing the state diagram to be simulated, otherwise we will not obtain the HMI panel.

We will add a frame, a few buttons, pushbuttons and other indicators.

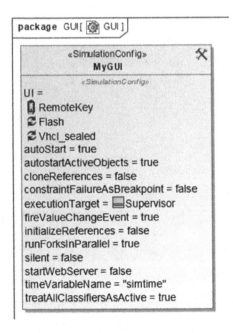

Figure 5.9. *Creation of the profile*

The first operation will therefore be the creation of the frame, then the assignment of the block containing the state machine to the created frame. True to my wish to not turn this book into a tutorial, we will not describe these steps in detail. The user guide, including an example of CSM, is sufficiently complete.

To assign a behavior to our buttons, we will drag and drop.

For example, for Locking, from the state diagram "LatchMangmt", we select the trigger Lck_Cmd, signal type (symbolized by a rectangle with orange background with an S). We drag and drop it on the button.

We will choose from the parameters, the execution target to specify the scope of the model to which the simulation will be applied.

Here we will choose only the block supporting the state diagram "LatchMangmt".

NOTE.– If a block contains parts with a multiplicity other than one, the simulator will create as many instances of the HMI and as many instances of the parts, including the underlying behaviors, the values of each instance will be accessible in the debugger.

The figure below illustrates this functionality, there are six locking instances for our case study (this might vary depending on the vehicle configuration, this is the typical default value), four for doors, one for the trunk and one for the fuel hatch.

In the following figure, we zoomed in on the different values of instances, also note the different active states. Each of the instances thus lives "its life" independently of the others, which for our example is interesting, notably to simulate a fault on one of the locks (engine failing, door badly closed, etc.), among the six that will actually be used in the real system. Before going into this level of detail, it will of course be necessary to ensure that the modeling and simulation effort justifies the specification contribution.

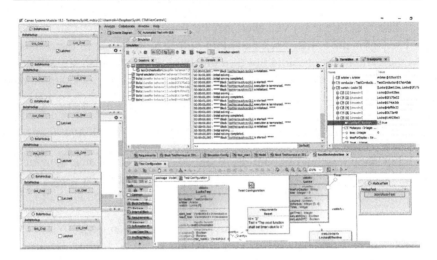

Figure 5.10. *Control of instances by the simulator*

Figure 5.11. *Zoom into the different instance values*

5.1.3. *Automated testing*

In the SysML toolbox, some diagrams can be used to describe test suites in order to stimulate the system, the results can be analyzed interactively, which is preferred for "unit tests"; however, when the model starts, to be quite comprehensive, it may be interesting to compare the expected results with the actual results, to automate the stimuli to perform regression tests etc.

The most advisable way to build an automated test configuration with CSM is to create a template dedicated to this purpose. To do this, we will use a CSM feature to reference a model from another. The idea will be to consider this new model as an overall system under test (SUT). In other words, this system will interact with our global model to stimulate system inputs, measure the output states and finally control the application of stimuli and the execution.

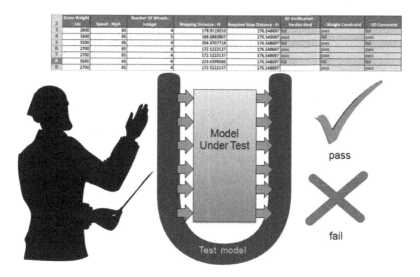

Figure 5.12. *Testing automation. For a color version of this figure, see www.iste.co.uk/casse/sysml.zip*

Our new model will consist of a main block with the SUT property. The test pattern generation scenario is provided by an activity diagram serving as a description of the overall test process, in which several sequence diagrams will apply stimuli at a programmed timing.

5.1.4. *Types of diagrams supported in simulation*

Most diagrams are supported, however the interest for some of them is limited, for example package diagrams. Clearly all those used for the behavioral description are supported, sometimes even with several uses: this is the case of the sequence diagram, which can serve as stimulus generator and as a means of execution trace.

Below is a table showing the execution possibilities of SysML diagrams.

Type of diagram	Executable	Standard	Comments
Requirements	Indirectly		For values
Use case	Indirectly		To simulate the sd under the uc
Sequence	YES	UMLTesting profile	Input AND Output
Package	N/A		It does not really make sense
Block Definition	Indirectly		Simulate the behavior of the Block
Internal Block	Ports & Flows		To follow the signals exchanged
Parametric	YES	OMG^{tm} SysML	Update constraints
State Machine	YES	W3C SCXML	Visited and current states
Activity	YES	OMG^{tm} fUML	The heart of the MBT solution

Table 5.1. *Diagrams animated by Cameo Systems Modeler*

NOTE.– The action language is left free in SysML as a reminder. CSM offers different executable languages according to JSR223 (see section 1.17.7).

5.1.4.1. *About the standards used in simulation*

5.1.4.1.1. SysML (parametrics with OMG)

Integrated in the SysML standard, SysML constraint blocks specify the physical properties or performance of a system. Model simulations can evaluate and display size, weight, speed, power, temperature and other parameters, throughout the life cycle of the system. Some tools integrate external mathematical solvers, by third-party tools. As is the case with CSM, however, CSM has also been offering an integrated solver in some versions.

5.1.4.1.2. SCXML (using W3C)

SCXML is the acronym for State Chart XML, which is a machine-based notation of states for the abstraction of their control. This includes a generic runtime environment based on David Harel's Statecharts. Used to describe event systems, control systems, in particular. These diagrams can be used for code generation.

5.1.4.1.3. fUML (foundational UMLwith OMG)

The following can be read on the OMG website:

> Semantics of a basic executable UML subset for UML executable models including a virtual machine for executing UML activities for verification. FUML supports the structural and behavioral semantics of systems through a subset of the UML meta-model.

5.1.4.1.4. JSR223

One of the most advanced features of Java 6 is the ability to integrate scripting languages with the JVM. From now on, it is possible to import scripts written with other languages in Java. This also includes the ability to pass Java objects to scripts and be able to manipulate them. Scripting languages can import Java classes, instantiate objects and use them. CSM based on a Java VM allows to use these different variants of scripts like language of action.

The JSR 223 specification allows embedding scripting languages in Java applications, and accessing and manipulating Java objects from the scripting environment. The supported languages are: Groovy, JRuby, Jython, Beanshell and Javascript.

5.1.4.2. *Animation*

This is the technique that allows most behavioral diagrams to visualize the current context: current state of a state machine, action executed in an activity diagram or message exchanged in a sequence diagram.

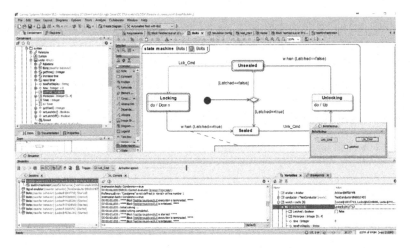

Figure 5.13. *Animation of a state diagram controlling locking*

A video illustrating this functionality on the YouTube channel of Olivier is recommended. It can be found by searching the keywords: YouTube Olivier CASSE MBSE.

5.1.5. *Execution trace*

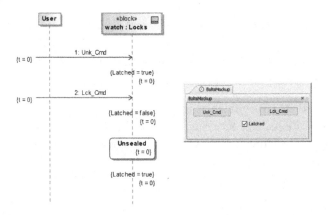

Figure 5.14. *Trace in the form of a sequence diagram*

5.1.6. *Generation of documents*

CSM offers several templates for exporting documents, which can of course be customized.

In the process of collaborative exchanges to understand and validate the system, the most relevant and accessible export is likely to be the SysML Web Report, generating in HTML navigable format documentation of the model.

This set of files can be shared by the Cameo Collaborator module, or by FTP in order to make it available on an intranet or completely accessible on the Internet, which is our case, having no privacy aspect to protect on our system.

Writing a specification document is an art, writing a template in order to generate from a template that kind of document is a challenge!

However, No Magic with CSM provides a very large number of templates which can be adapted in order to create a template corresponding perfectly to your needs.

Among the available templates, one can see availability of a version compliant with the standard IEEE − 1233, the System Requirements Specification report, also known as SysRS, available online on the No Magic MBSE blog.

Glossary

Abstract block: A block that cannot be directly instantiated. Contrast: concrete block.

Abstraction: An abstraction is a relationship that relates two elements or sets of elements that represent the same concept at different levels of abstraction or from different viewpoints.

Action: An action is a named element that is the fundamental unit of executable functionality. The execution of an action represents some transformation or processing in the modeled system, be it a computer system or otherwise.

Active object: An object that may execute its own behavior without requiring method invocation. This is sometimes referred to as "the object having its own thread of control". The points at which an active object responds to communications from other objects are determined solely by the behavior of the active object and not by the invoking object. This implies that an active object is both autonomous and interactive to some degree. See: active class, thread.

Activity: An activity is the specification of parameterized behavior as the coordinated sequencing of subordinate units whose individual elements are actions.

Activity diagram: A diagram that depicts behavior associated with activities using input/output and control flow.

Activity final node: An activity final node is a final node that stops all flows in an activity.

Activity node: An activity node is an abstract class for points in the flow of an activity connected by edges.

Activity parameter node: An activity parameter node is an object node for inputs and outputs to activities.

Activity partition: An activity partition is a kind of activity group for identifying actions that have some characteristic in common.

Actor: An actor specifies a role played by a user or any other system that interacts with the subject (the term "role" is used informally here and does not necessarily imply the technical definition of that term found elsewhere in this specification).

Actual parameter: Synonym: argument.

Aggregate: A class that represents the "whole" in an aggregation (whole-part) relationship. See: aggregation.

Aggregation: A special form of association that specifies a whole-part relationship between the aggregate (whole) and a component part. See: composition.

Allocate: A mapping between from one set of model elements (supplier) to another set of model elements (client). The mapping is often performed as part of the design process to refine the design. Typical examples of allocation include allocation of functions to components, logical to physical components, flows to connectors and software to hardware. The allocation of requirements to components is generally accomplished using the SysML satisfy relationship. See: allocated element, allocate activity partition, allocate behavior, allocate flow and allocate structure.

Allocated element: A stereotype of an element that is the client or supplier of an allocation with properties allocated from or allocated to. See: allocation.

Apply: A relationship that is used to stereotype a model element.

Association: An association describes a set of tuples whose values refer to typed instances. An instance of an association is called a link.

Attribute: A structural feature of a classifier that characterizes instances of the classifier. An attribute represents a declared state of one or more instances in terms of a named relationship to a value or values. See also: property.

Behavior: Behavior is a specification of how its context classifier changes state over time. This specification may be either a definition of possible behavior execution or emergent behavior, or a selective illustration of an interesting subset of possible executions. The latter form is typically used for capturing examples, such as a trace of a particular execution. A behavior can take a number of forms: interaction, state machine, activity, or procedure (a set of actions).

Behavioral feature: A behavioral feature is implemented (realized) by a behavior. A behavioral feature specifies that a classifier will respond to a designated request by invoking its implementing method.

Binary association: An association between two blocks. A special case of an n-ary association.

Boolean: A boolean type is used for logical expression, consisting of the predefined values true and false.

Block: A modular unit that describes the structure of a system or element.

Block definition diagram: A diagram that represents the relationship between blocks and the structural and behavioral features of blocks.

Block property: A property of a block that enables the unit, dimension and distribution capabilities to be applied and enforces additional constraints specific to SysML. The Block property is abstract.

Boolean expression: An expression that evaluates to a boolean value.

Call action: Call action is an abstract block for actions that invoke behavior and receive return values.

Call behavior action: Call behavior action is a call action that invokes a behavior directly rather than invoking a behavioral feature that, in turn, results in the invocation of that behavior.

Call operation action: Call operation action is an action that transmits an operation call request to the target object, where it may cause the invocation of associated behavior.

Cardinality: The number of elements in a set. Contrast: multiplicity.

Child: In a generalization relationship, the specialization of another element, the parent. See: sub block, subtype. Contrast: parent.

Choice pseudo state: A pseudo state which, when reached, result in the dynamic evaluation of the guards of the triggers of its outgoing transitions.

Classifier: A classifier is a classification of instances, it describes a set of instances that have features in common.

Classification: The assignment of an instance to a classifier. See dynamic classification, multiple classification and static classification.

Client: A classifier that requests a service from another classifier. Contrast: supplier.

Combined fragment: A combined fragment defines an expression of interaction fragments. A combined fragment is defined by an interaction operator and corresponding interaction operands. Through the use of combined fragments the user will be able to describe a number of traces in a compact and concise manner.

Comment: A comment is a textual annotation that can be attached to a set of elements.

Communication path: An association between a use case and an actor.

Composite: A block that is related to one or more blocks by a composition relationship. See: composition.

Composite aggregation: See composition.

Composite state: A state that consists of either concurrent (orthogonal) sub states or sequential (disjoint) sub states. See: sub state.

Composition: A form of aggregation which requires that a part instance be included in at most one composite at a time, and that the composite object is responsible for the creation and destruction of the parts. Composition may be recursive. Synonym: composite aggregation.

Concrete block: A block that can be directly instantiated. Contrast: abstract block.

Concurrency: The occurrence of two or more activities during the same time interval. Concurrency can be achieved by interleaving or simultaneously executing two or more threads. See: thread.

Concurrent sub state: A sub state that can be held simultaneously with other sub states contained in the same composite state. See: composite state. Contrast: disjoint sub state.

Condition: A boolean expression which is true as long as the expression evaluates true, and is false otherwise. See: guard condition.

Connector: Specifies a link that enables communication between two or more instances. This link may be an instance of an association, or it may represent the possibility of the instances being able to communicate because their identities are known by virtue of being passed in as parameters, held in variables or slots, or because the communicating instances are the same instance.

Connector end: A connector end is an endpoint of a connector, which attaches the connector to a connectable element. Each connector end is part of one connector.

Constraint: A constraint is a condition or restriction expressed in natural language text or in a machine readable language for the purpose of declaring some of the semantics of an element.

Constraint block: A block that packages the statement of a constraint so it may be applied in a reusable way to properties of other blocks. A constraint block includes the definition of one or more constraint parameters which can be bound to properties in a specific context where the constraint is used.

Constraint parameter: A property of a constraint block that is used to bind other properties in a specific context where the constraint is used.

Constraint property: A block property that is typed by a constraint block, and owned by a containing block. A usage of a constraint block in a particular context that can constrain other properties (e.g. value properties).

Containment: See namespace containment.

Containment hierarchy: A namespace hierarchy consisting of model elements, and the containment relationships that exist between them. A containment hierarchy forms a graph.

Continuous rate: A sub block of rate which enables a parameter value to be sampled at an infinite rate (e.g. the increment of time between parameter values approaches zero). See: rate, discrete rate.

Control flow: A control flow is an edge that starts an activity node after the previous one is finished.

Control input: An input that activates or deactivates a function. See: activation, activation/deactivation event.

Control node: A control node is an abstract activity node that coordinates flows in an activity. It is used to coordinate the flows between other nodes. It covers initial node, final node, and its children, fork node, join node, decision node, and merge node.

Control operator: A behavior that is intended to represent an arbitrarily complex logical operator that can be used to enable and disable other actions.

Control value: An enumerated value that is used to control the execution of an activity. See: control operator.

Copy: A relationship between a supplier requirement that represents the orignal and a client requirement that represents a copy of the original.

Data type: A type whose instances are identified only by their value. A data type may contain attributes to support the modeling of structured data types.

Decomposition: A description of a whole in terms of its component parts. See: aggregation.

Decision node: A decision node is a control node that chooses between outgoing flows.

Deep history state: A pseudo state that represents the most recent active configuration of the composite state that directly contains this pseudo state (e.g., the state configuration that was active when the composite state was last exited).

Delegation: The ability of an object to issue a message to another object in response to a message. Delegation can be used as an alternative to inheritance. Contrast: inheritance.

Dependency: A dependency is a relationship that signifies that a single or a set of model elements requires other model elements for their specification or implementation. This means that the complete semantics of the depending elements is either semantically or structurally dependent on the definition of the supplier element(s).

Derive requirement: A dependency relationship between two requirements in which a client requirement can be generated or inferred from the supplier requirements or additional design information. Derived requirements may refine or restate a requirement to improve stakeholder communications or to track design evolution.

Derived: A requirement that has been derived from another requirement. A requirement that one or more components of a system must satisfy. Note: This term is sometimes used to refer to a constraint on the design process versus the system. See: requirement.

Destruction event: A destruction event models the destruction of an object.

Diagram: A graphical presentation of a collection of model elements, most often rendered as a connected graph of arcs (relationships) and vertices or nodes (other model elements).

Diagram description: A comment that provides standardized information about a diagram. See: reference data.

Diagram usage: A form of stereotype applied to a diagram to constrain its use. See: diagram.

Dimension (Unit): A kind of quantity that may be stated by means of defined units. For example, the dimension of length may be measured by units of meters, kilometers, or feet. See: dimension, unit, value type and value property.

Discrete rate: A subclass of rate which enables a parameter value to be sampled at a finite rate (e.g. the increment of time between parameter values is non zero). See: rate, continuous rate.

Disjoint sub state: A sub state that cannot be held simultaneously with other sub states contained in the same composite state. See: composite state. Contrast: concurrent sub state.

Distribution definition: A probability distribution that may be specified on a block property. Synonym probability distribution. See: distribution result.

Do action domain: An area of knowledge or activity characterized by a set of concepts and terminology understood by practitioners in that area.

Duration: A duration defines a value specification that specifies the temporal distance between two time expressions that specify time instants.

Duration constraint: A duration constraint defines a constraint that refers to a duration interval.

Duration interval: A duration interval defines the range between two durations.

Effectiveness measure: A criterion for system optimization that is critical to the success of the mission. Note: The criterion are often used to support trade studies to select among alternatives well as to optimize a given design. See measure of effectviness. production, deployment, support, and disposal systems.

Enhanced functional flow block diagram: A restricted form of activity diagram. See: activity diagram.

Entry action: An optional behavior of a state that is executed whenever the state is entered regardless of the transition taken to reach the state. If defined, entry actions are always executed to completion prior to any internal behavior or transitions performed within the state.

Entry point: A pseudo state that is an entry point of a state machine or composite state. In each region of the state machine or composite state it has a single transition to a vertex within the same region.

Enumeration: An enumeration is a data type whose values are enumerated in the model as enumeration literals.

Environment: A collection of systems and items that interact either directly or indirectly with the system of interest. See: item, system.

Event: An event is the specification of some occurrence that may potentially trigger effects by an object. Or a noteworthy occurrence that occurs at the instant of time when a specified expression evaluates true.

Exception: A special kind of signal, typically used to signal fault situations. The sender of the exception aborts execution and execution resumes with the receiver of the exception, which may be the sender itself. The receiver of an exception is determined implicitly by the interaction sequence during execution; it is not explicitly specified.

Execution: The state of the system or model when it is running. For a model, this implies that model computation is occurring.

Execution specification: An execution specification is a specification of the execution of a unit of behavior or action within the Lifeline.

Exit action: An optional behavior that is executed whenever this state is exited regardless of which transition was taken out of the state. If defined, exit actions are always executed to completion only after all internal activities and transition actions have completed execution.

Exit point: A pseudo state that is an exit point of a state machine or composite state. Entering an exit point within any region of the composite state or state machine referenced by a submachine state implies the exit of this composite state or submachine state and the triggering of the transition that has this exit point as source in the state machine enclosing the submachine or composite state.

Expression: An expression represents a node in an expression tree, which may be non-terminal or terminal. It defines a symbol, and has a possibly empty sequence of operands that are value specifications.

Extend: A relationship from an extending use case to an extended use case that specifies how and when the behavior defined in the extending use case can be inserted into the behavior defined in the extended use case. See extension point, include.

Extension: An extension is used to indicate that the properties of a metaclass are extended through a stereotype, and gives the ability to flexibly add (and later remove) stereotypes to blocks.

Extension point: An extension point identifies a point in the behavior of a use case where that behavior can be extended by the behavior of some other (extending) use case, as specified by an extend relationship.

Failure: An inability to satisfy a requirement. See: requirement.

Feature: A behavioral or structural characteristic of a classifier.

Final Node: A final node is an abstract control node at which a flow in an activity stops.

Final state: A special kind of state signifying that the enclosing region is completed. If the enclosing region is directly contained in a state machine and all other regions in the state machine also are completed, then it means that the entire state machine is completed.

Fire: To execute a state transition. See: transition.

Flow final node: A flow final node is a final node that terminates a flow.

Flow property: A property of a flow specification or a block that signifies a single flow element to/from a Block.

Focus of control: A symbol on a sequence diagram that shows the period of time during which an object is performing an action, either directly or through a subordinate procedure.

Fork node: A fork node is a control node that splits a flow into multiple concurrent flows.

Formal parameter: Synonym: parameter.

Function: A transformation of inputs to outputs that may include the creation, monitoring, modification or destruction of elements, or a null transformation.

Functional requirement: A function that must be performed. See: requirement.

Generalization: A generalization is a taxonomic relationship between a more general classifier and a more specific classifier. Each instance of the specific classifier is also an indirect instance of the general classifier. Thus, the specific classifier inherits the features of the more general classifier. See: inheritance.

Guard condition: A condition that must be satisfied in order to enable an associated transition to fire. See: condition.

Hardware: A component of a system that has geometric constraints. See: component.

Implementation: A definition of how something is constructed.

operations defined for the type with the same behavior as specified for the type's operations. See: type.

Import: An element import identifies an element in another package, and allows the element to be referenced using its name without a qualifier. A package import is a relationship that allows the use of unqualified names to refer to package members from other namespaces. Contrast: export.

Include: An include relationship defines that a use case contains the behavior defined in another use case. See: extend.

Information flow: An information flow specifies that one or more information items circulate from its sources to its targets. Information flows require some kind of "information channel" for transmitting information items from the source to the destination. An information channel is represented in various ways depending on the nature of its sources and targets.

Information item: An information item is an abstraction of all kinds of information that can be exchanged between objects. It is a kind of classifier intended for representing information at a very abstract way, which cannot be instantiated.

Inheritance: See generalization.

Initial node: An initial node is a control node at which flow starts when the activity is invoked.

Initial pseudo state: An initial pseudo state represents a default vertex that is the source for a single transition to the default state of a composite state. There can be at most one initial vertex in a region. The initial transition may have an action.

Input/output: An item that is subject to a transformation by a function. See: argument, function port, parameter and signature.

Instance: An entity that has unique identity, a set of operations that can be applied to it, and state that stores the effects of the operations. See: object.

Instance specification: An instance specification is a model element that represents an instance in a modeled system.

Integer: A whole number.

Interaction: An interaction is a unit of behavior that focuses on the observable exchange of information between connectable elements. An emergent behavior that results from two or more dependent behaviors. Note: A system or component interacts with other components its environment, to yield an emergent system behavior from the individual component behaviors.

Interaction operator: Interaction Operator is an enumeration designating the different kinds of operators of combined fragments. The interaction operand defines the type of operator of a combined fragment. The literal values of this enumeration are: alt, assert, consider, critical, ignore, loop, neg, opt, par, seq and strict.

Interface: An interface is a kind of classifier that represents a declaration of a set of coherent public features and obligations. An interface specifies a contract; any instance of a classifier that realizes the interface must fulfill that contract. The obligations that may be associated with an interface are in the form of various kinds of constraints (such as pre- and postconditions) or protocol specifications, which may impose ordering restrictions on interactions through the interface. The inputs, outputs, ports, connections, connecting components (i.e. harness) and associated information that support one or more interactions between systems. An interface in systems engineering is generally more broadly defined consistent with the SysML. See: provided interface, required interface.

Interface requirement: An interface a system must support. See: requirement.

Internal block diagram: A diagram that depicts the internal structure of a block, including the interaction points to other parts of the system. It shows the configuration of parts that jointly perform the behavior of the containing block. The diagram specifies a set of instances playing parts (roles) in the context of the enclosing block (context).

Internal transition: A transition signifying a response to an event without changing the state of an object interruptible activity region. An interruptible activity region is an activity group that supports termination of tokens flowing in the portions of an activity.

Item flow: Representation of the items that flow across a connector or an association that is a subclass of a directed relationship (Note: more precisely a subclass of information flow) that is realized by a relationship that conveys the item(s). See: item, item property.

Item property: A property that relates the instances of the item to the instances of its enclosing class. See: item, item flow and property.

Iteration loop: A specialized loop where the loop repeats a specified number of times.

Join node: A join node is a control node that synchronizes multiple flows.

Junction pseudo state: Junction pseudo states are semantic-free vertices that are used to chain together multiple transitions. They are used to construct compound transition paths between states.

Lifeline: A lifeline represents an individual participant in the interaction.

Link: An instance of an association. See: association.

Manual procedure: A set of operations that provide instructions for a user to perform. See: procedure.

Mean: The expected value associated with a probability distribution.

Measure of effectiveness: See effectiveness measure, objective function.

Merge node: A merge node is a control node that brings together multiple alternate flows. It is not used to synchronize concurrent flows but to accept one among several alternate flows.

Message: A message defines a particular communication between lifelines of an interaction.

Meta class: A class whose instances are classes. Meta classes are typically used to construct meta models.

Meta-meta model: A model that defines the language for expressing a meta model. The relationship between a meta-meta model and a meta model is analogous to the relationship between a meta model and a model.

Meta model: A model that defines the language for expressing a model.

Metaobject: A generic term for all metaentities in a metamodeling language. For example, metatypes, metaclasses, meta-attributes and meta-associations.

Method: The implementation of an operation. It specifies the algorithm or procedure associated with an operation.

Model: It is an abstraction of the physical system, with a certain purpose. This purpose determines what is to be included in the model and what is irrelevant.

Model element: A constituent of a model that is an abstraction drawn from the system being modeled.

Model interchange: The ability to exchange model information.

Model library: A stereotyped package that contains model elements that are intended to be reused by other packages. A model library differs from a profile in that a model library does not extend the metamodel using stereotypes and tagged definitions. A model library is analogous to a class library in some programing languages.

Multiple inheritance: A semantic variation of generalization in which a type may have more than one supertype. Contrast: single inheritance.

Multiplicity element: A multiplicity is a definition of an inclusive interval of non-negative integers beginning with a lower bound and ending with a (possibly infinite) upper bound. A multiplicity element embeds this information to specify the allowable cardinalities for an instantiation of this element. Contrast: cardinality.

Name: A string used to identify a model element.

Named element: A named element is an element in a model that may have a name.

Namespace: A namespace is an element in a model that contains a set of named elements that can be identified by name. See: name.

Namespace containment: See containment.

Need: A desired requirement of a stakeholder. See: requirement.

Nested connector end: A connector end that allows a connected property to be identified by a multi-level path through a part (property) hierarchy.

Note: See comment.

Notation: The graphical depiction of a model construct.

Object flow: An object flow is an activity edge that can have objects or data passing along it.

Object node: An object node is an abstract activity node that is part of defining object flow in an activity.

Operation: An operation is a behavioral feature of a classifier that specifies the name, type, parameters and constraints for invoking an associated behavior.

Operational requirement: A requirement which is associated with the operation of a system, and typically includes a combination of functional, interface and performance requirements. See: requirement.

Optional parameter: A stereotype of a parameter with lower multiplicity equal to zero indicating that the parameter is not required for the activity to begin execution. Otherwise, the lower multiplicity must be greater than zero, which is call "required". (See required parameter, activity parameter node). Synonym non-triggering input.

Package: A package is used to group elements, and provides a namespace for the grouped elements.

Package containment: See namespace containment.

Package diagram: A diagram that depicts how model elements are organized into packages and the dependencies among them, including package imports and package extensions.

Parameter: A parameter is a specification of an argument used to pass information into or out of an invocation of a behavioral feature. Synonyms: formal parameter. Contrast: argument.

Parameter set: A parameter set is an element that provides alternative sets of inputs and outputs that a behavior may use.

Parametric diagram: A diagram that represents a network of constraints on properties to support engineering analysis such as performance, reliability and mass properties analysis.

Parent: In a generalization relationship, the generalization of another element, the child. See: subclass, subtype. Contrast: child.

Part: An element representing a set of instances that are owned by a containing classifier instance. (See role.) Parts may be joined by attached connectors and specify configurations of linked instances to be created within an instance of the containing classifier. Note: This is referred to as a part property in SysML which is an owned property of a block. See: property.

Participate: The connection of a model element to a relationship or to a reified relationship. For example, a class participates in an association, an actor participates in a use case.

Partition: A grouping of any set of model elements based on a set of criteria:

1) Activity diagram: A grouping of activity nodes and edges. Partitions divide the nodes and edges to constrain and show a view of the contained nodes. Partitions can share contents. They often correspond to organizational units in a business model. They may be used to allocate characteristics or resources among the nodes of an activity.

2) Architecture: A set of related classifiers or packages at the same level of abstraction or across layers in a layered architecture. A partition represents a vertical slice through an architecture, whereas a layer represents a horizontal slice. Contrast: layer.

Performance property: A measure of the transformation or response of a function or behavior (i.e. response time, etc.).

Performance requirement: A performance property a system must satisfy. See: requirement.

Physical property: A physical characteristic of a system or element (i.e. weight, color).

Physical requirement: A physical property a system must satisfy. See: requirement.

Pin: A pin is an object node for inputs and outputs to actions. See: function port input/output.

Port: A port is a property of a classifier that specifies a distinct interaction point between that classifier and its environment or between the (behavior of the) classifier and its internal parts. The part of a system or component that provides access between a system's behaviors and properties and its environment. Note: This is sometimes referred to as an interaction point.

Postcondition: A constraint expresses a condition that must be true at the completion of an operation.

Precondition: A constraint expresses a condition that must be true when an operation is invoked.

Primitive type: A primitive type defines a predefined data type, without any relevant substructure (i.e., it has no parts). A primitive datatype may have an algebra and operations defined outside of SysML, for example, mathematically.

Probability: Note: used in activities.

Probability distribution: A mathematical function which defines the likelihood of a particular set of outcomes. See: expression.

Problem: A deficiency, limitation, or failure to satisfy a requirement or need, or other undesired outcome. Note: A problem may be associated with the behavior, structure, and/or properties of a system or element at any level of the hierarchy (i.e. system of system level, down to a component/part level). See: need, requirement.

Problem cause: The relationship between a problem and its source problems (i.e. cause). Note: This cause effect relationship is often represented in fishbone diagrams, fault trees, etc.

Procedure: A set of actions that may be attached as a unit to other parts of a model, for example, as the body of a method. Conceptually a procedure, when executed, takes a set of values as arguments and produces a set of values as results, as specified by the parameters of the procedure.

Profile: A profile defines limited extensions to a reference metamodel with the purpose of adapting the metamodel to a specific platform or domain.

Property: A property is a structural feature. A usage of a class that relates the instances of the enclosing class to the instances of the class that types the property.

Pseudo-state: A pseudo-state is an abstraction that encompasses different types of transient vertices in the state machine graph.

Rate: A specification of the number of objects and values that traverse the edge per time interval, that is, the rate they leave the source node and arrive at the target node. See: discrete rate and continuous rate.

Rationale: An element that documents the principles or reasons for a modeling decision, such as an analysis choice or a design selection. It provides or references the basis for the modeling decision and can be attached to any model element.

Real: A value type that represents a real number which can have a value from negative infinity to infinity.

Realization: Realization is a specialized abstraction relationship between two sets of model elements, one representing a specification (the supplier) and the other represents an implementation of the latter (the client). Realization can be used to model stepwise refinement, optimizations, transformations, templates, model synthesis, framework composition, etc.

Receive: The handling of a stimulus passed from a sender instance. See: sender receiver.

Receiver: The object handling a stimulus passed from a sender object. Contrast: sender.

Reception: A declaration that a classifier is prepared to react to the receipt of a signal.

Reference: 1) A denotation of a model element. 2) A named slot within a classifier that facilitates navigation to other classifiers. Synonym: pointer.

Reference property: A property of a block that refers to another element of a system or system description, but is not owned by the block.

Refine: A relationship that represents a fuller specification of something that has already been specified at a certain level of detail. For example, a design class is a refinement of an analysis class.

Region: A region is an orthogonal part of either a composite state or a state machine. It contains states and transitions.

Relationship: Relationship is an abstract concept that specifies some kind of relationship between elements.

Required interface: Contrast: provided interface.

Required parameter: A parameter that is required for the activity to begin execution. The lower multiplicity must be nonzero. See: optional parameter, activity parameter node.

Requirement: a capability or condition that must (or should) be satisfied.

Requirement traceability: The relationship between a source requirement and the derived requirements needed to satisfy the source requirement. See: requirement, derive and trace.

Requirement type: A category of requirement. Note: This includes functional, interface, performance, etc.

Requirements diagram: A diagram that represents requirements and their relationships. See: requirement.

Resource: Any element that is needed for the execution of a function. See: resource constraint.

Role: The named set of features defined over a collection of entities participating in a particular context:

– Collaboration: The named set of behaviors possessed by a class or part participating in a particular context.

– Part: a subset of a particular class which exhibits a subset of features possessed by the class.

– Associations: A synonym for association end often referring to a subset of classifier instances that are participating in the association.

Run time: The period of time during which a computer program or a system executes.

Satisfy: A dependency relationship between a requirement and a model element that fulfills the requirement. See: derive, verify.

Scalable: A measure of the extent to which the modeling language (or methodology, etc.), can be adapted to an increase in scope and/or complexity.

Scenario: A specific sequence of actions that illustrates behaviors. A scenario may be used to illustrate an interaction or the execution of a use case instance. See: interaction.

Semantics: The meaning of a model element. Note: a precise meaning should be able to be expressed mathematically.

Send [a message]: The passing of a stimulus from a sender instance to a receiver instance. See: sender, receiver.

Sender: The object passing a stimulus to a receiver instance. Contrast: receiver.

Sequence diagram: A diagram that depicts an interaction by focusing on the sequence of messages that are exchanged, along with their corresponding event occurrences on the lifelines.

Unlike a communication diagram, a sequence diagram includes time sequences but does not include object relationships. A sequence diagram can exist in a generic form (describes all possible scenarios) and in an instance form (describes one actual scenario). Sequence diagrams and communication diagrams express similar information, but show it in different ways. See: communication diagram.

Shallow history state signal: A signal is a specification of type of send request instances communicated between objects.

Simple state: A state that does not have nested states. See: state, composite state.

Slot: A slot specifies that an entity modeled by an instance specification has a value or values for a specific structural feature.

Software: A component of a system that specifies instructions which are executed by a computer. See: component.

Source requirement: The requirement which is the basis for deriving one or more other requirements.

Specialized requirement: A requirement that is not explicitly addressed by the default requirement types. Note: This may include safety, reliability, maintainability, producibility, usability, security, etc.

Specification: A set of requirements for a system or other element.

Stakeholder: Individuals, groups, and/or institutions which may be impacted by the system throughout its life cycle, including acquisition, development, production, deployment, operations, support and disposal.

State: A state models a situation during which some (usually implicit) invariant condition holds. A condition of a system or element, as defined by some of its properties, which can enable system behaviors and/or structure to occur. Note: The enabled behavior may include no actions, such as associated with a wait state. Also, the condition that defines the state may be dependent on one or more previous states.

State invariant: A state invariant is a runtime constraint on the participants of the interaction.

State machine diagram: A diagram that depicts discrete behavior modeled through finite state-transition systems. In particular, it specifies the sequences of states that an object or an interaction goes through during its life in response to events, together with its responses and actions. See: state machine.

State machine: State machines can be used to express the behavior of part of a system. Behavior is modeled as a traversal of a graph of state nodes interconnected by one or more joined transition arcs that are triggered by the dispatching of series of (event) occurrences. During this traversal, the state machine executes a series of activities associated with various elements of the state machine.

Stereotype: A stereotype defines how an existing metaclass may be extended, and enables the use of platform or domain specific terminology or notation in place of, or in addition to, the ones used for the extended metaclass.

Stimulus: The passing of information from one instance to another, such as raising a signal or invoking an operation. The receipt of a signal is normally considered an event. See: message.

Streaming: A property of a parameter that specifies whether its values can be accepted or produced by an action while executing. A non-streaming parameter specifies that the parameter value can only be accepted at the beginning of execution and produced at the end of execution. Contrast: non streaming.

String: A string is a sequence of characters in some suitable character set used to display information about the model. Character sets may include non-Roman alphabets and characters.

Subblock: In a generalization relationship, the specialization of another class, the superblock. See: generalization. Contrast: superblock.

Submachine state: A state in a state machine that is equivalent to a composite state but whose contents are described by another state machine.

Substate: A state that is part of a composite state. See: concurrent state, disjoint state.

Subpackage: A package that is contained in another package.

Subsystem: A unit of hierarchical decomposition for large systems. A subsystem is commonly instantiated indirectly. Definitions of subsystems vary widely among domains and methods, and it is expected that domain and method profiles will specialize this construct. A subsystem may be defined to have specification and realization elements.

Subtype: In a generalization relationship, the specialization of another type, the supertype. See: generalization. Contrast: supertype.

Superblock: In a generalization relationship, the generalization of another class, the subclass. See: generalization. Contrast: subclass.

Supertype: In a generalization relationship, the generalization of another type, the subtype. See: generalization. Contrast: subtype.

Supplier: A classifier that provides services that can be invoked by others. Contrast: client.

Synch state: A vertex in a state machine used for synchronizing the concurrent regions of a state machine.

System: An organized set of elements functioning as a unit. An item, with structure, that exhibits observable properties and behaviors. See: block, part, component and item.

System (component) boundary: The set of all ports, which connect the system (component) to its environment.

System hierarchy: A decomposition of a system and its components.

System interconnection: The connection between systems and components. See: connector.

Tagged value: The explicit definition of a property as a name-value pair. In a tagged value, the name is referred as the tag. Certain tags are predefined in the SysML others may be user defined. Tagged values can be properties of a stereotype. See: constraint, stereotype.

Test case: A method that is used to verify a requirement has been satisfied. See requirement, satisfy and verify. Note: A test case in SysML is intended to be consistent with a test case in the UML testing profile.

Text-based requirement: One or more requirements specified in text. See: requirement.

Time constraint: A time constraint defines a Constraint that refers to a TimeInterval.

Time event: A time event specifies a point in time. At the specified time, the event occurs. See: event.

Time expression: A time expression defines a value specification that represents a time value.

Time property: A property of the model that represents a local or global time, which other properties may depend on. Note: The property can support continuous or discrete-time models. This variable should not be confused with the measured or computed time that an actual system uses, which depends on a number of implementation specific factors related to clocks, synchronization, etc. See: property.

Time reference: The time property from which other time properties are derived. See: time property.

Trace: A dependency that indicates a historical or process relationship between two elements that represent the same concept without specific rules for deriving one from the other. Trace dependencies are used to track requirements and changes across models.

Trade-off analysis: An evaluation of alternatives based on a set of evaluation criteria.

Transition: A transition is a directed relationship between a source vertex and a target vertex. It may be part of a compound transition, which takes the state machine from one state configuration to another, representing the complete response of the state machine to an occurrence of an event of a particular type. Response to events/ conditions, which triggers a behavior.

Trigger: A trigger relates an event to a behavior that may affect an instance of the classifier.

Triggering input: An input which is required for a function to be activated. See: required parameter.

Type: A stereotyped class that specifies a domain of objects together with the operations applicable to the objects, without defining the physical implementation of those objects. A type may not contain any methods, maintain its own thread of control, or be nested. However, it may have attributes and associations. Although an object may have at most one implementation class, it may conform to multiple different types. See: implementation class. Contrast: interface.

Type expression: An expression that evaluates to a reference to one or more types.

Unit: A standard for expressing a quantity in terms of the magnitudes of other quantities that have the same dimension. A unit often relies on precise and reproducible ways to measure the unit. For example, a unit of length such as a meter may be specified as a multiple of a particular wavelength of light. See: dimension, value property.

Usage: A dependency in which one element (the client) requires the presence of another element (the supplier) for its correct functioning or implementation.

User: An individual or group of individuals that use a system. See: actor.

Use case: A use case is the specification of a set of actions performed by a system, which yields an observable result that is, typically, of value for one or more actors or other stakeholders of the system. See: use case instances.

Use case diagram: A diagram that shows the relationships among actors and the subject (system), and use cases.

Value property: A property of a block that holds a value. See: value type.

Value type: A type that defines values.

Verdict: The outcome of executing one or more test cases or verification procedures. See test case, verification procedure, verification result, verify. Note: This term is borrowed from the testing profile.

Verification: The process for demonstrating a system satisfies its requirements.

Verification procedure: The functions needed to support execution of a test case. Note. This may include generating an input stimulus and monitoring an output response. See: procedure, manual procedure.

Verification result: The outcome of executing one or more test cases. See: verdict.

Verification system: The system that implements the verification procedures.

Verified: A named element that verifies a requirement.

Verify: A relationship between a requirement and a test case that can determine whether a system satisfies the requirement. See: requirement, test case and verdict.

Vertex: A source or a target for a transition in a state machine. A vertex can be either a state or a pseudo-state. See: state, pseudo-state.

View: A view is a representation of a whole system from the perspective of a single viewpoint. See model.

View point: A view point is a specification of the conventions and rules for constructing and using a view for the purpose of addressing a set of stakeholder concerns.

Visibility: An enumeration whose value (public, protected, or private) denotes how the model element to which it refers may be seen outside its enclosing namespace.

Bibliography

[ALB 08] ALBINET A., BEGOC S., BOULANGER J.-L. *et al.*, "The MeMVaTEx methodology: from requirements to models in automotive application design", *4th European Congress ERTS (embedded real time software)*, Toulouse, France, March 2008.

[BAD 14] BADREAU S., BOULANGER J.L., *Ingénierie des exigences*, Dunod, Paris, 2014.

[CAS 05] CASSE O., Présentation de SysML V0.9 par Artisan SW Tools, AFIS, April 2005.

[CAS 10a] CASSE O., REIS-MONTEIRO M., "A ReqIF/SysML profile example – Requirements exchange and roundtrip", *ERTS Congress*, Toulouse, France, January 2010.

[CAS 10b] CASSE O., HAUSE M., Assessing Quality in SysML Models, May 2010.

[COC 00] COCKBURN A., *Writing Effective Use Cases*, Addison-Wesley, Boston, 2000.

[DOJ 03] US DEPARTMENT OF JUSTICE, "Information Ressource Management", available at: www.justice.gov/archive/jmd/irm/lifecycle/table.htm, 2003.

[FRI 08] FRIEDENTHAL S., MOORE A., STEINER R., *A Practical Guide to SysML*, Morgan Kaufmann, San Francisco, 2008.

[HAR 87] HAREL D., GERY E., "Statecharts: a visual formalism for complex systems", available at: http://www.inf.ed.ac.uk/teaching/courses/seoc/2005_2006/resources/statecharts.pdf, 1987.

[HAU 05] HAUSE M., "SysML – making UML more effective for systems engineers", *IEE Seminar on UML Systems Engineering*, January 2005.

[ISO 08] ISO, Systems and Software Engineering – Software Lifecycle Processes, ISO/IEC 15288:2008, 2008.

[ISO 11] ISO, Systems and software engineering – Systems and software Quality Requirements and Evaluation (SQuaRE) – Evaluation process, ISO/IEC 25040:2011, 2011.

[IRE 12] IREB, Professionnel certifié en ingénierie des exigences, Syllabus, 2012.

[LUZ 13] LUZEAUX D., RUAULT J.R., *L'ingénierie système*, AFNOR, 2013.

[NFE 13] NF EN 16271, Management par la valeur – Expression fonctionnelle du besoin et cahier des charges fonctionnel – Exigences pour l'expression et la validation du besoin à satisfaire dans le processus d'acquisition ou d'obtention d'un produit, AFNOR, February 2013.

[OMG 06] OBJECT MANAGEMENT GROUP (OMG), SysML-v1-Glossary-06-03-04, (OMG SysML™) Version 0.98, April 2006.

[OMG 16] OBJECT MANAGEMENT GROUP (OMG), "Semantics of a Foundational Subset for Executable UML Models (FUML™)", available at www.omg.org/spec/FUML/1.2.1, January 2016.

[OMG 17] OBJECT MANAGEMENT GROUP (OMG), OMG SysML Modeling language, (OMG SysML™) Version 1.5, May 2017.

[ROQ 13] ROQUES, P., *Modélisation de systèmes complexes avec SysML, Eyrolles*, Paris, 2013.

[W3C 15] W3C, State Chart XML (SCXML): State Machine Notation for Control Abstraction, W3C recommendation, September 2015.

Index

Printed in the United States
By Bookmasters